REPTILE

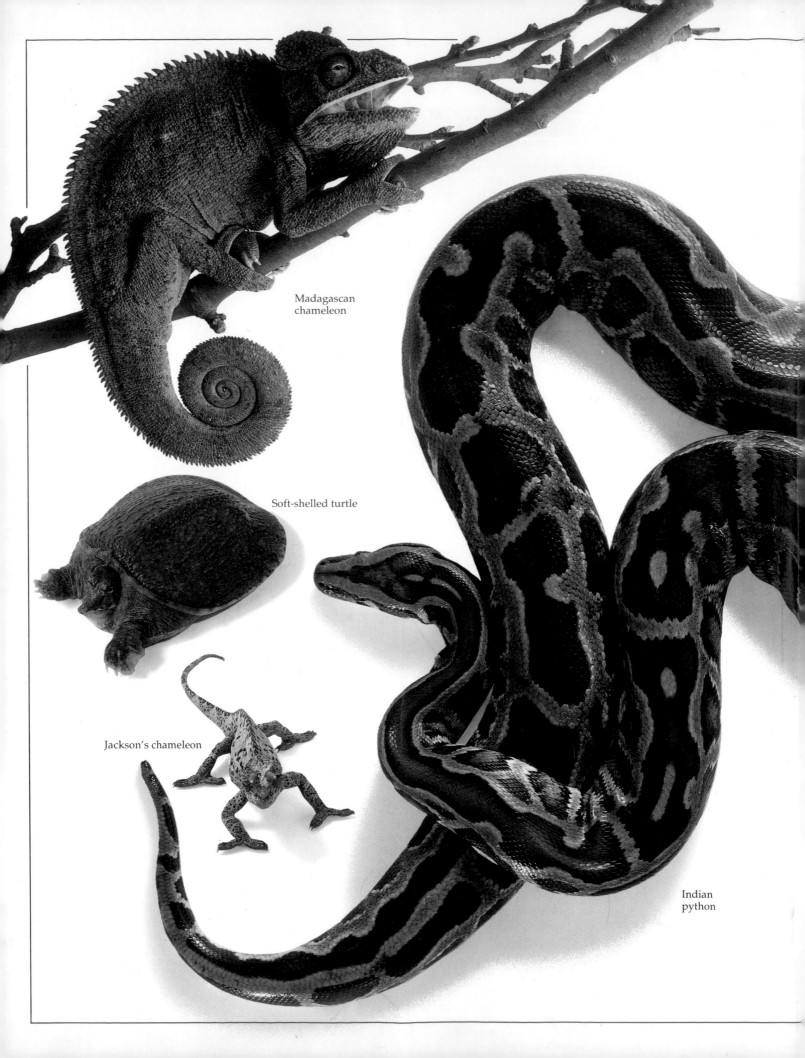

Madagascan
chameleon

Soft-shelled turtle

Jackson's chameleon

Indian
python

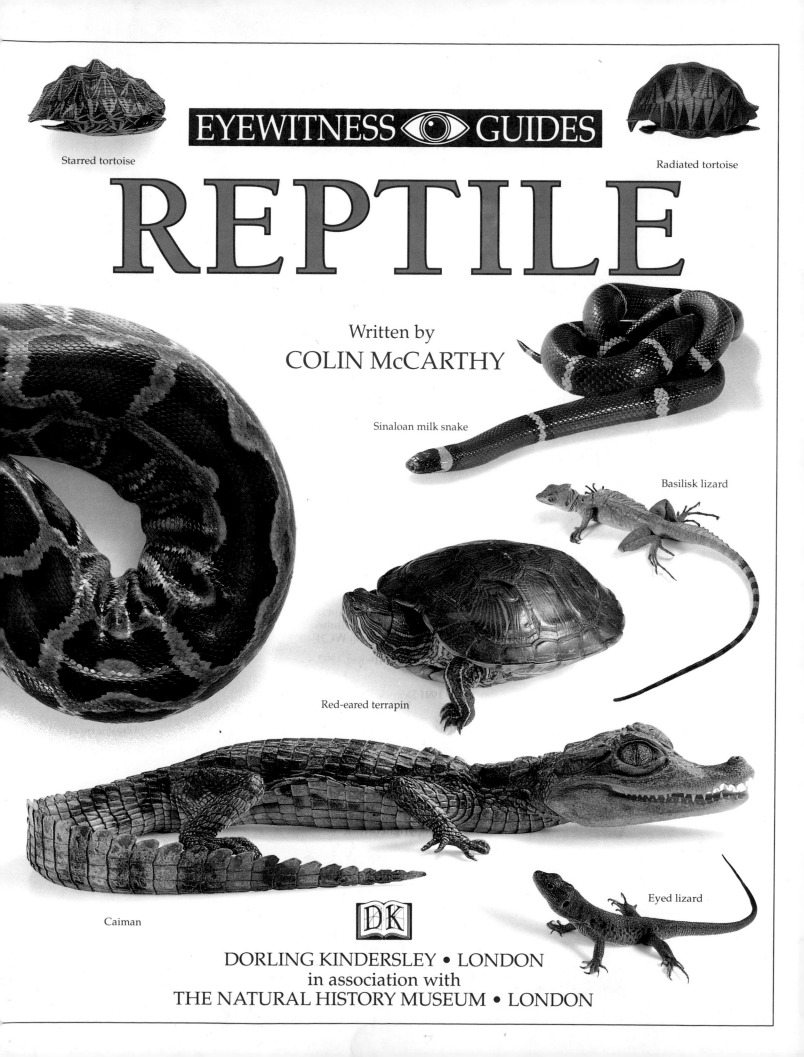

Starred tortoise

Radiated tortoise

EYEWITNESS 👁 GUIDES

REPTILE

Written by
COLIN McCARTHY

Sinaloan milk snake

Basilisk lizard

Red-eared terrapin

Caiman

Eyed lizard

DK

DORLING KINDERSLEY • LONDON
in association with
THE NATURAL HISTORY MUSEUM • LONDON

Tree skink

Tegu lizard

Caiman

Grass snake

Flying snake

Alligator snapping turtle

Corn snake

DK

A DORLING KINDERSLEY BOOK

Project editors Gillian Denton, Lynne Williams
Art editor Neville Graham
Senior editor Helen Parker
Senior art editors Jacquie Gulliver, Julia Harris
Production Louise Barratt
Picture research Kathy Lockley
Special photography Karl Shone, Jane Burton,
Kim Taylor, Colin Keates

This Eyewitness Guide has been
conceived by Dorling Kindersley Limited
and Editions Gallimard

First published in Great Britain in 1991
by Dorling Kindersley Limited,
9 Henrietta Street, London WC2E 8PS

Reprinted 1993 (twice), 1997

A CIP catalogue record for this book is available
from the British Library

ISBN 0-86318-576-2

Colour reproduction by Colourscan, Singapore
Typeset by Windsor Graphics, Ringwood, Hampshire
Printed and bound in Singapore by Toppan Printing Co. (S) Pte Ltd.

Contents

Rat snake

What is a reptile?

THERE ARE FOUR GROUPS of reptiles alive today: snakes and lizards, the crocodile family, turtles and tortoises, and the tuatara. Reptiles, like fish, amphibians, birds, and mammals are vertebrates (they have backbones), and their young are usually born on land. However, when reptiles hatch from their eggs they look like mini-versions of their parents. Reptiles have a scaly skin which is good at keeping in body moisture so that they can live in dry places, but it is less successful at retaining body heat. Thus, reptiles depend on their surroundings for warmth. Although known as cold-blooded, the blood of a sun-warmed reptile is about the same temperature as ours. Warm-blooded creatures have to eat frequently to maintain their body temperature, and waste energy looking for food. Reptiles do not need to eat to keep warm and so survive well in barren areas.

Scaly skin

DREAMY DRAGONS
Reptiles, have featured in the mythology of many countries for hundreds of years. The dragons illustrated here were described by Marco Polo, the famous Italian explorer, who had possibly seen huge species of lizards and snakes on his travels. The winged dragons were probably inspired by flying lizards he had seen in the east. The evil, multi-headed hydra grew two heads when one was cut off. In Greek legend, Hercules finally killed the beast by cauterizing each neck as the head was cut off.

Hydra

Extra long toe for added support

What is not a reptile?

At first glance, the salamander looks like a lizard, however, it is not a reptile but an amphibian. Amphibians, which include frogs and toads, are often mistaken for reptiles, although they belong to a different group of animals. They are unlike reptiles in many ways. They have no scales because they need to breathe through their skin. This is kept moist by special mucus glands. Most frogs, toads, and salamanders also need to be near water when they breed. They often lay eggs straight into water where the tadpoles then hatch. This European fire salamander, however, keeps her eggs inside her body until seconds before hatching, when she gives birth to tadpoles straight into the water.

Fire salamander

Like all frogs, this monkey frog is an amphibian. Unlike reptiles, most frogs have smooth, moist skin and no scales.

External ear

Tail helps balance

Eye with movable eyelid

Many reptiles have special tongues

TEGU LIZARD
Reptiles come in all sorts of shapes and sizes. Lizards are one of the biggest and most varied groups. Tegu lizards come from tropical South America. This is quite a young tegu, but as tegus age, they get fatter from their diet of young birds, mammals, and even other lizards. A tegu's skin is covered with horny, dead scales which are good at keeping in its body fluids. Its eyes are well-developed, but in other reptiles, particularly burrowing lizards or snakes, they may be much smaller. The tegu's eyelids are movable like most other lizards. However, some geckos and most snakes cannot blink, as their eyes are protected by a solid, transparent "spectacle". The feet of many reptiles give a good clue to the animals' life – style. They may be used for clambering over smooth surfaces, climbing among swaying stems, or negotiating hot, soft sand dunes. Some burrowing lizards and most snakes have no legs.

LAYING ON LAND
Most reptiles lay eggs (pp. 20–21), although there are some that give birth to live young. Unlike most amphibians, reptiles lay their eggs on land. This includes the reptiles which normally spend a great deal of their life in the water, like turtles and crocodiles. Reptiles lay their eggs in a great variety of sites - on river banks, in sand, in termite mounds, in grasses. The incubation period changes from one reptile to another and is affected by climate.

African grass snake with eggs

7

When reptiles ruled the world

reptiles owe their success mainly to their special eggs (pp. 6–7)

PTEROSAURS
Flying reptiles, or pterosaurs, dominated the air for over 100 million years, until they became extinct at the same time as the dinosaurs. Their wings were membranes stretched between a single long finger and their legs.

THE FIRST REPTILE APPEARED some 340 million years ago during the time known as the Carboniferous period. They evolved from amphibians, and although not much is known of their very early history, it seems likely that these first reptiles looked like some of our lizards today. It was not until the later Mesozoic era, 230 to 70 million years ago, that the flying reptiles appeared. During this period other reptiles gave up living on land and returned to dominate the seas and lakes, and the dinosaurs ruled the land. The reptiles owe their success mainly to their special eggs (pp. 6–7) which, unlike those of the amphibians, usually have shells, and do not need water. The reptiles themselves were therefore more adaptable and able to use habitats which would be unsuitable for water-dependent amphibians.

Vertebra of *Palaeophis*, an ancient sea snake

ANCIENT GIANTS
The enormous vertebrae of an extinct form of sea snake, known as *Palaeophis*, found in West Africa, proved the existence in the Caenozoic era of a snake three to four times the size of a modern python. The vertebra shown here is from a present-day python over 6 m (2 ft) long. Although stories of 20 m (65 ft) long ancient snakes have been reported, these are likely to be mythical.

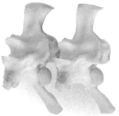
Vertebra of a modern python

TIME CHART OF THE EARTH (Millions of years ago)					
Palaeozoic era		Mesozoic era			Caenozoic era
Carboniferous period	Permian period	Triassic period	Jurassic period	Cretaceous period	Palaeocene period to the present day
350	270	225	190	141	70
Turtles, tortoises, and terrapins					
		Crocodilians			
		Lizards			
				Snakes	

Duration of each period not to scale

SLOW TO CHANGE
Lizards first appeared about 200 million years ago, evolving alongside dinosaurs. Although rare as fossils, there is evidence that different lizards existed before the end of the Mesozoic era. The example, which is 190 million years old, shows the small head, short neck, long body and tail, and sprawling legs that are still typical of the group today.

— *Pointed teeth for eating fish*

OLD CROCS
The crocodile is probably the closest living relative of the dinosaurs, and seems to have evolved at the same time during the Triassic period, about 200 million years ago. The sharp, pointed teeth of early forms suggest that they were mostly specialized fish-eaters, unlike most modern species, which may take in a little plant matter with their meat. The basic crocodile skull has changed little.

Ancient crocodile skull

DOG JAW

This skull with its dog-like jaws belonged to a meat-eating reptile called *Cynognathus*. This four-footed creature was an advanced form of the mammal-like reptiles, which dominated land animals through much of the Permian and Triassic periods. It was from this group of reptiles that mammals evolved about 195 million years ago.

Skull of *Cynognathus*

Strong jaw and large teeth for meat-eating

A reconstruction of an advanced mammal-reptile showing an improved non-sprawling posture

TURTLE FIRST

The fossilized remains of the first recognizable turtle were found in rocks some 200 million years old. Although never one of the dominating reptiles, the turtle's structure was flexible enough to cope with the many changes in the environment that have taken place since it evolved. This adaptability has allowed turtles to develop successful land and aquatic forms, and to become the oldest living group of reptiles.

TOOTHLESS

The skull of a modern turtle has no roof openings and there are no teeth in the jaws (pp. 32–33). The skull of *Proganochelys*, which dates from the early Triassic period, shows that the ceiling of the skull has not changed. There are, however, tooth-like projections in the roof of the mouth, although they are not visible here.

Toothless jaws

Happy families

EVOLUTION IS THE BASIS for the classification of animals. In the same way that you are related to your brothers and sisters because you share the same parents, and to your cousins because you share the same grandparents, animals are divided up into family groups according to their common ancestors. Lizards and snakes, therefore, are more closely related to each other than to any other group, but surprisingly, crocodiles are more closely related to birds than to other reptiles. However, because there is often not enough evidence about ancestors, family groupings also depend on the common features of the animals alive today (pp. 6–7).

REPTILES TODAY
Only four groups of reptiles have managed to survive until modern times. The largest by far are the lizards and the snakes. The others were not always so scarce; fossils of at least 108 species of crocodilians are known and the group to which the lone tuatara belongs were similarly more widespread in the past.

	Lizards 3,000 species
	Snakes 2,700 species
	Turtles 200 species
	Crocodilians 23 species
	Tuatara 1 species

Monitor lizard

LIZARDS
Lizards come in many different shapes and sizes. Iguanas, agamas, and chameleons are closely related to each other, and with geckos form the most primitive lizard group. Wall and sand lizards, whiptails and racerunners, girdle-tail lizards, and skinks are another closely related group. Monitors, beaded lizards, and glass lizards are also grouped together (pp. 28–29).

DAVID AND GOLIATH
The largest reptile in the world is the estuarine or saltwater crocodile. It commonly grows to a length of 5 m (16 ft) but individuals as long as 8 m (26 ft) have been recorded. It is an aggressive crocodile and is found from southern India to northern Australia. The smallest reptile in the world is the British Virgin Island gecko which is often no longer than 18 mm (0.7 in).

British Virgin Island gecko

Estuarine crocodile

SNAKES

Snakes are legless reptiles with long, slender bodies. There are three groups of snakes: primitive snakes, which include pythons and boas; blind snakes, which include thread snakes; advanced snakes which include rear-fanged snakes, cobras, sea snakes, and vipers. Snakes are found all over the world except in very cold areas (pp. 26–27).

Indian python

TURTLES

These are reptiles with short, broad bodies, enclosed in a bony shell. The bone of the shell is usually covered by horny plates, or less commonly, by leathery skin. Turtles are divided into two main groups according to the way the neck bends when the head retreats into the shell: the hidden-neck turtles include snapping turtles, terrapins, tortoises, sea turtles, and softshell turtles; the side-necked turtles include the snake-necked turtle, the matamata, and African mud turtles. Turtles and tortoises live on land, and in fresh or salt water (pp. 30–31).

Hermann's tortoise

CROCODILIANS

Crocodilians are divided into three families: crocodiles, gharials, and alligators, which includes caimans. They are a very old group of reptiles, and in several ways are more advanced than the other groups. They have a much more efficient blood circulation system and according to some, a more intelligent brain. They also show much greater care for their young (pp. 34–35).

Caiman

Inside out

IN MANY REPTILES, bone growth does not stop at maturity, which means that some reptiles keep growing throughout their lives. If a reptile survives the every-day dangers of life, it may eventually become giant–sized. This is particularly true of pythons, crocodiles, and the giant tortoises, although the smaller lizards and turtles normally do stop growing. When they are old, most reptiles do not lose their teeth as mammals do, but continue to shed and grow new ones (pp. 38–39).

Unlike a snake, the insides of a lizard are quite symmetrical

Tail vertebra

Trunk vertebra

Chameleon skeleton

Skull

Ribs

CHAMELEON
Many lizards have highly specialized skeletons. The chameleon, for example, is adapted for life in trees and bushes. The body is broad, providing greater stability when the animal's weight is centred over a narrow twig or branch (pp. 28–29). The fingers and toes are designed for grasping, especially grouped with three toes on the outside and two on the inside of the foot, and the other way round on the hand. The tail is prehensile, or tailor-made for grasping.

Caiman skeleton

Skull

Neck vertebra

Tail vertebra

CAIMAN
The caiman's skull is long, with the eye sockets and nostrils set high, so that the caiman can float with just its nose and eyes above the water. Its body is long as well, with two pairs of rather short legs, and five toes on the front feet and only four on the back. The toes on all the feet are partly webbed. The upper jaw of the caiman, as with all other members of the crocodile family, is almost solid bone.

Ribs

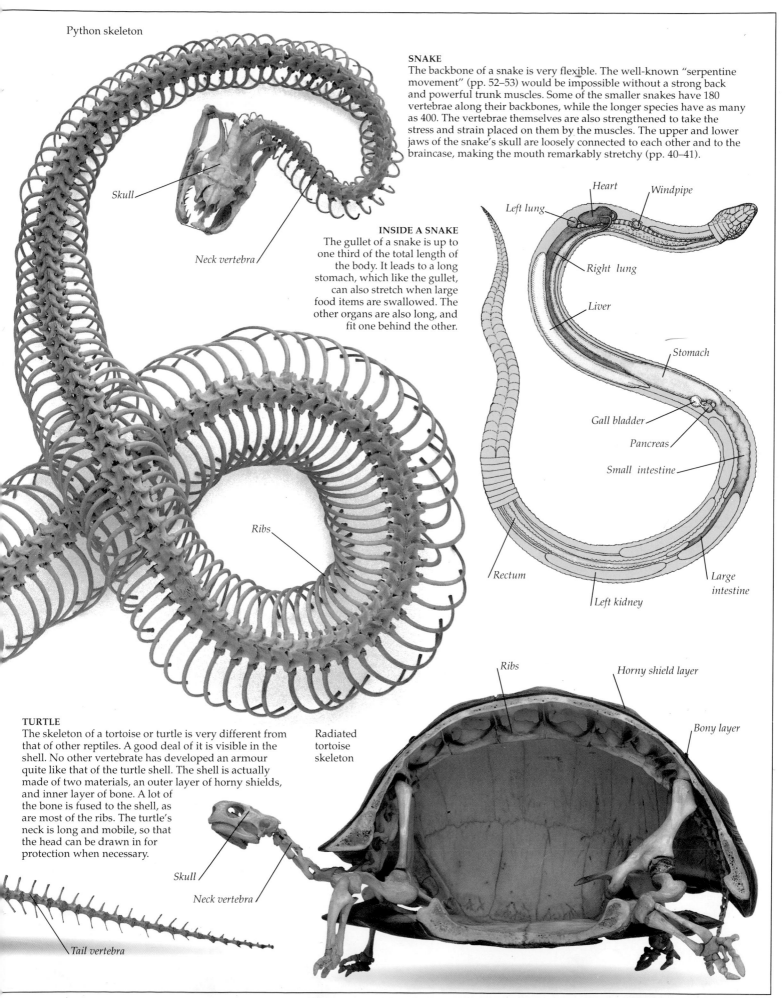

Python skeleton

Skull

Neck vertebra

Ribs

SNAKE
The backbone of a snake is very flexible. The well-known "serpentine movement" (pp. 52–53) would be impossible without a strong back and powerful trunk muscles. Some of the smaller snakes have 180 vertebrae along their backbones, while the longer species have as many as 400. The vertebrae themselves are also strengthened to take the stress and strain placed on them by the muscles. The upper and lower jaws of the snake's skull are loosely connected to each other and to the braincase, making the mouth remarkably stretchy (pp. 40–41).

INSIDE A SNAKE
The gullet of a snake is up to one third of the total length of the body. It leads to a long stomach, which like the gullet, can also stretch when large food items are swallowed. The other organs are also long, and fit one behind the other.

Heart

Windpipe

Left lung

Right lung

Liver

Stomach

Gall bladder

Pancreas

Small intestine

Large intestine

Left kidney

Rectum

Ribs

Horny shield layer

Bony layer

TURTLE
The skeleton of a tortoise or turtle is very different from that of other reptiles. A good deal of it is visible in the shell. No other vertebrate has developed an armour quite like that of the turtle shell. The shell is actually made of two materials, an outer layer of horny shields, and inner layer of bone. A lot of the bone is fused to the shell, as are most of the ribs. The turtle's neck is long and mobile, so that the head can be drawn in for protection when necessary.

Radiated tortoise skeleton

Skull

Neck vertebra

Tail vertebra

13

Cool customers

Rᴇᴘᴛɪʟᴇꜱ ᴀʀᴇ ᴄᴏʟᴅ-ʙʟᴏᴏᴅᴇᴅ (pp. 6–7). This means that their temperature changes with that of their surroundings. Although they live best where the climate is hot, it takes time for them to adjust to rapid temperature changes. To speed the process, they often warm up by basking in the sunshine, and as they get warm, they may start moving in search of food, or even a mate. As the day becomes hotter, they move into the shade to cool down. By shuttling backwards and forwards, in and out of the shade, they keep a surprisingly constant internal temperature. High temperatures are needed when the reptile is digesting food; for instance a snake that has fed, but cannot get to the heat, may die because the food in its stomach will be too cold. In poor weather, reptiles have low body temperatures, and so they will be slow-moving and in danger from predators.

Lizard basking in the heat

KEEPING COOL
In the early morning this agama lizard will sit on top of the rock in the bright sunlight. When it reaches the temperature it likes best, it runs around looking for insects to eat, but in the hottest part of the day it will retreat into the shade. If it cools down too much it will creep back on to the rock. The pattern of warming and cooling down varies with the seasons. For example, during the cool months reptiles are only active at midday, when it is warm, but during the summer months they may go underground at midday to avoid overheating.

Sand lizard

HOT FOOT
When the ground is too hot for its feet, the sand lizard of the Namib Desert "dances", lifting its legs up alternately from the scorching sand. Sometimes, it rests on its belly, lifting all four legs up at the same time! The little ground gecko is also uncomfortable on the hot sand, but is mainly nocturnal, so would normally be out when it is cooler.

Ground gecko

TAKING IT EASY
Crocodiles cool down by letting moisture evaporate through their opened mouths. They warm up in water in cold weather, and use it as a refreshing dip in the heat. Some crocodiles simply lie in the cool waters of a muddy stream, but the American crocodiles lie in burrows or holes when they find the heat too much.

BOILING OVER
Some people go red with anger as blood rushes to their face, but their blood temperature does not really rise. Committing a deed "in cold blood" refers to a callous action, and is a misunderstanding of the term (pp. 6–7).

TAKING COVER
Like many other desert snakes, the sand viper will do its best to avoid the full heat of the day. It is mainly nocturnal, moving in a "sidewinding" fashion as it hunts for prey (pp. 52–53). It may travel as much as 1 km (half a mile) in a single night, searching for its favourite food – small mammals and lizards. If it needs to escape the hot midday sun of the deserts of North Africa and Arabia, it simply sinks itself into the sand.

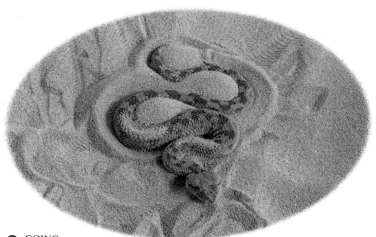

2 GOING...
The snake descends vertically, shuffling and rocking its body. As it goes down, it shovels sand upwards and over its back. The scales along the snake help to work the grains of sand along its body.

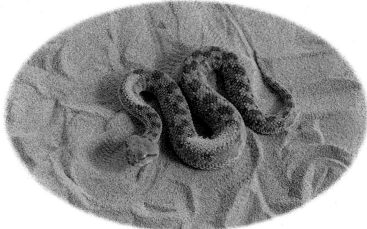

1 GOING...
A sand viper retreats into the sand, tail first, wriggling as it goes. Its eyes are well protected from irritating grains of sand by the solid "spectacles" that cover and shield them.

3 GONE!
The sand viper is now almost completely buried. Soon only the top of its head will be visible. Bedding down in the hot desert sand in this way protects it from the scorching sun, and at the same time, makes a perfect hiding place when either enemies or prey are nearby.

Snake leaves very visible marks as it moves in the sand

Uncommon senses

Reptiles have senses common to vertebrates – smell, sight and hearing. They also have a number of additional ways of finding out about their surroundings. Snakes, and some lizards, "smell" with the help of the tongue and the sensory cells in the roof of their mouth, called the Jacobson's organ. Some snakes are very sensitive to infra-red heat rays, which means they can detect warm-blooded prey, even in total darkness. Marine turtles can navigate immense distances to their nesting beaches. They may use the position of the sun, but it is also possible that they can sense magnetic fields. In some reptiles, certain senses are not very highly developed. Most of the burrowing types, for instance, have poor eyesight, and snakes cannot hear very well, but many other reptiles have good hearing.

ALLIGATOR ROAR
Alligators communicate with one another over vast distances by bellowing. The sound can be very loud, up to 92 decibels at 5 m (16 ft), roughly as loud as the propeller engine of a small aeroplane!

Swivelling eye is set on a turret

Eyelids can close to tiny peepholes

Special toes grasp branches like pincers

SMALL BUT NOISY
Most geckos have a voice. Certain species produce chirping and clicking noises, usually when mating or defending their territories. When distressed, some even produce ultrasounds. These are detectable by mammals or birds, but are out of the hearing range of the lizards themselves, who use them to alarm predators.

BROAD HORIZONS
The chameleon has an extraordinarily wide field of vision and can move its eyes independently. If it sees a fly, it can keep one eye in that direction, while it manoeuvres itself towards its prey. As it moves, the other eye scans the surroundings, keeping a look-out for possible enemies. The chameleon's brain then has the job of interpreting the two different images. When the fly is in range, the chameleon swivels both eyes towards it, and at this point its eyesight becomes more like the binocular vision of humans. With both eyes firmly fixed on the fly, the chameleon can judge its position more accurately – and prepare to take aim.

SENSITIVE SOULS

Like all animals, snakes have gradually changed, or evolved, over millions of years. At some point they seem to have gone through a burrowing stage which affected their senses. Their eyesight and hearing became weaker, while other senses became more acute. Snakes have no external ears, and vibrations simply move along to the inner ear through skull bones that are joined to the lower jaw. Some snakes have special heat detectors. This Indian python has little heat sensitive holes (pits) in its lips. These are particularly useful for detecting warm-blooded prey, such as mammals or birds, at night (pp. 42–43).

MUSIC TO ITS EARS

For thousands of years, snakes have been shown dancing to the music of a charmer's pipe. This has led to the mistaken belief that the snakes are somehow hypnotized by the music. In fact, the snake is rising in defence and following the movement of the pipe as it prepares to attack it.

Deeply forked tongue

Eye has "glassy" stare because there is no movable eyelid

TESTING THE AIR

All lizards have a well-developed, extendable tongue and the tongues of snakes and monitor lizards are deeply forked. They flick in and out, constantly sipping or "tasting" chemical particles in the air or on the ground. These particles are transferred from the tip of the tongue to the Jacobson's organ in the roof of the mouth. The organ, or series of cells, partly "smells" and partly "tastes" these particles. This specialized tongue can help to trail prey, sample food, find a mate, and detect enemies.

Nostril

Jacobson's organ

Tongue

Tear duct

Eye is protected by transparent solid "spectacles"

SIGHT AND SOUND

Iguanas have very good eyesight. They can see in colour, which explains why many members of the iguana family communicate by using their colourful head ornaments, crests, and throat fans. In fact, colour is important in many lizards as it is a way of distinguishing between the sexes. Whereas snakes mainly hear vibrations from the ground through their skull bones, iguanas, and most lizards, can hear air-borne sounds through visible ear openings. The ear drum is nearly level with the surrounding skin, while in mammals it is found in a deep "ear hole". Although a typical lizard can hear better than a snake, it cannot hear as well as a human.

Dating displays

ALTHOUGH REPTILES SPEND most of their time in day-to-day survival, adjusting body heat, searching for food, or escaping from predators, they do need to develop a social life. Most obviously in the mating season, they need to be able to attract members of the opposite sex, in order to reproduce. Male lizards often display bright colours to appeal to the female, and the more ornate features of some, such as frills and crests, are also there for the same purpose. As in the rest of the animal world, the males may use the same signals that are meant to attract females to warn off male rivals.

BIRTH CONTROL
Many snakes can delay egg fertilization, in some cases for months after they have mated. This ability to control the development of young is very handy. In fact, the old woman of the British nursery rhyme, "who had so many children, she didn't know what to do", would have benefited from the same technique.

FLASHY
The male frigate bird attracts his mate in very much the same way as the anole lizard. He keeps his pouch inflated for several hours – in fact until she succumbs to his charms.

A COUPLE OF SWELLS
Anole lizards are highly territorial. The males display regularly to one another, inflating their brilliant reddish throat sacs as a sign of aggression. Two lizards of the same size may flaunt this brightly coloured flap of skin at one another for hours at a time, although a smaller lizard will retreat immediately if threatened in this way. Anole lizards come from the tropical areas of South and Central America where there are many different species. They are sometimes called "American chameleons", although they are really iguanas. They climb around in green and brown vegetation, where they blend in well with their surroundings. This helps to protect them from their enemies.

SPRING IN THE AIR
Giant tortoises mate in the spring, when the male will often ram the female in the side with his shell to show his interest. The act of mating sometimes takes several hours.

SNAKE CHARMERS
Once a male snake has successfully found a female, he approaches her, then stimulates her into mating by rubbing his chin along her back, while their bodies and tails intertwine. During the mating season, two male snakes will sometimes perform a kind of combat dance, as they vie for a particularly favoured female. Reptiles often avoid the need to fight by signalling at a distance. The contest is less a test of strength (during which one or both snakes may be injured) than an opportunity to prove which creature is superior.

MAY THE BEST MAN WIN
Male monitors wrestle at the beginning of the mating season, rearing up on their hind legs. The weaker animal finally gives up, usually before it is injured.

Tails intertwined during mating

Throat sac inflated to attract female or as a sign of aggression

Examining eggs

Y OUNG REPTILES DEVELOP inside an egg cushioned in a bag of fluid called the amnion. The eggs of most reptiles have a soft and flexible shell, although some have hard shells rather like birds' eggs. Oxygen and moisture, necessary for the young reptile's growth and development, is absorbed through the shell, while the yolk provides it with food. Some lizards and snakes are viviparous, that is they give birth to fully developed young.

Snakes

The eggs of most snakes have parchment-like shells. The young hatch by slashing a hole in the shell, using a special sharp egg tooth. Most snakes bury their eggs in a little soil or in rotting vegetation. Several vipers, boas, and sea snakes, however, are viviparous.

Ground python egg

Indian python egg

UNDERGROUND COVER
Scarcely recognizable as an egg, this extraordinary-looking object was laid by a ground python, a burrowing snake from West Africa. The egg is large in proportion to the mother. A female 85 cm (33 in) may lay eggs 12 cm (4 in) in length.

MOTHER LOVE
After laying about 30 of these leathery-shelled eggs, the female Indian python takes unusual care of her precious brood, coiling herself round her eggs. By continuously twitching her muscles (rather like shivering) she raises the temperature within the coils several degrees higher than her surroundings.

COMMON AS MUCK
The common African house snake often chooses manure heaps or termite mounds in which to lay its eggs, usually eight or ten at a time.

African house snake egg

FACT OR FICTION?
In Greek mythology, there are many tales about a tribe of war-like women, called the Amazons, who hated men and lived without them. In fact, some all-female lizards, like the little whiptail, can also reproduce without mating.

Whiptail lizard

Monitor lizard egg

Lizards

Most lizards produce eggs with leathery shells, apart from geckos which tend to lay hard-shelled eggs. Most lizards are not good mothers and ignore their eggs once they have been laid. Some skinks, however, return to their nests to brood, raising the temperature of the eggs with their bodies.

African chameleon eggs

Javan bloodsucker egg

STUCK ON YOU
The tokay gecko, like many geckos and skinks, lays eggs two at a time. The eggs are soft and sticky at first, but they soon harden when exposed to the air. As the eggs dry, they stick to the surface on which they were laid.

Tokay gecko eggs

BURIED ALIVE
Some chameleons give birth to live young, while others lay eggs. The African chameleon, which lives in trees, comes down to the ground to lay its clutch of 30 – 40 eggs in a burrow. The chameleon fills this in to protect the eggs, so that when the young hatch, they have to dig themselves out.

SPINDLE EGGS
The eggs of the tree-dwelling Javan bloodsucker, an agamid lizard, are a most peculiar, spindle shape. It is not clear why this is, because closely related species have normal, oval eggs.

CUCKOOS IN THE NEST
The Nile monitor lizard likes to lay her eggs in termite mounds. She tears a hole in the side of the mound and then lays 40 – 60 eggs . The heat inside the mound helps to incubate the eggs which hatch after nine or ten months.

Crocodilians

Caimans and alligators make mound nests out of fresh vegetation, soil, and leaf litter for their hard-shelled eggs, while crocodiles and gharials make hole nests in exposed beaches and dry, crumbly soil. The female often stays near the nest, to stop would-be thieves from raiding it. All crocodilian eggs have to be kept warm. In fact, the sex of the hatchling is determined by minute temperature changes during the early stages of incubation.

Dwarf crocodile egg

Alligator egg

LENDING A PAW
The female American alligator builds a mound of plant-matter and soil, then digs a hole in it to lay 35 – 40 eggs. When the eggs have hatched and the young alligators are ready to leave the nest, they grunt loudly and their mother tears open the nest.

LITTLE MYSTERY
The African dwarf crocodile is basically nocturnal. It lays fewer eggs than most other crocodiles – less than 20 – but they are quite large and are laid directly into a specially constructed mound.

WHO'S EATING WHOM?
Man and crocodile live side by side along the coast of Papua New Guinea. This shield shows a figure inside the crocodile's belly. The people of Papua New Guinea believed that crocodiles held magical powers.

Turtles and tortoises

Tortoises, and some turtles, lay hard-shelled eggs, but the egg shells of marine and some river turtles are soft. Most females make a hole in the ground for their eggs and they may return to the same spot year after year. As with crocodiles, the sex of baby turtles and tortoises is often determined by the temperature during incubation.

Spur-thighed tortoise egg

Snake-necked turtle egg

Matamata egg

MATAMATA
The eggs of this strange, South American turtle look very much like ping-pong balls. Like all aquatic turtles, the matamata must leave the water to lay her eggs. These turtles were previously hunted for their meat, but they are now protected.

MEDITERRANEAN MATES
The spur-thighed tortoise is found all round the Mediterranean. Up until recently it was also exported in large numbers to pet shops in northern European countries. Few of them survived this experience. Importing them is now against the law in most places.

SNAKE-NECKED TURTLE
The Australian snake-necked turtle leaves the water to lay her eggs in a nest that she digs on dry land. She lays her eggs at night, after rainfall.

Galapagos tortoise egg

GENTLE GIANT
The Galapagos giant tortoise is one of the biggest in the world. It lays its hard-shelled eggs in soil that is exposed to the sun. The eggs are sometimes incubated for 200 days. Unfortunately, many are destroyed by foraging rats and pigs, which were introduced to the islands by humans.

MASS NESTING
Every year some 200,000 Ridley sea turtles come to Orissa, India, to nest along just 5 km (3 miles) of beach. Each female digs a hole in which she lays about 100 eggs, then she returns to the sea.

ADDED PROTECTION
Like birds' eggs, reptilian eggs have a shell which protects the developing young, but also allows it to breathe. The shell is made up of several layers. Here the brittle outer layer has been broken, revealing a flexible inner layer. Under this is the amniotic membrane which fills with fluid, creating a suitable environment for the growing embryo.

Shell allows embryo to breathe

Embryo

Amnion

Yolk sac

Spitting images

Baby reptiles are born as small versions of their parents. Whether they hatch from eggs (pp. 20–21) or are born live, they are able to feed themselves, and live in much the same environment as they will do when they are fully grown. They naturally change their feeding habits as they develop, as their growing body demands more food. A young crocodile, for example, may be able to survive on insects, but, as it grows bigger, it will eat considerably larger prey, including mammals, birds, and fish. Unlike most amphibians, reptiles do not come into the world in a larval or tadpole state (pp. 6–7), nor do they have a completely different life-style and diet from the adult. They are not born in a weak and immature condition and do not depend upon their parents to feed them and care for them, as is the case with most mammals and birds.

Young caiman

LIKE MOTHER LIKE DAUGHTER
This young caiman meets the world fully formed and able to fend for itself. Like the young alligator, it will stay close to its mother for a few weeks, sometimes using her back as a basking platform. Despite the mother's care, unusual in reptiles, at the first sign of danger the young are able to dive under water for cover.

HATCHING OUT
Once they are laid, snake eggs often swell and get heavier as they absorb moisture from the environment (pp. 20–21), but the length of time needed before they hatch varies according to the temperature. The warmer it is, the faster the eggs develop, so the parent often chooses to lay them in a place that is both warm and slightly moist. Piles of vegetation produce heat as the plant material rots, so compost heaps are sometimes selected as nesting sites, particularly by snakes living in cooler areas. Often the hatchling or young snake that emerges is much longer than the egg it hatched from. This is possible because as the embryo develops, the whole body is coiled into a tight spiral.

1 THE EGG
This is the egg of a rat snake, a common and rather large snake from North America. Its mating season is from April to June and also in the autumn. Between June and August the female lays 5 to 30 soft-shelled, oblong eggs, often choosing rotten wood, leaf litter, or a spot under some rocks as her "nest".

4 MAKING A MOVE
The snake leaves the egg quite quickly. It is able to slither along in the normal snake-like way immediately (pp. 52–53). Interestingly, however, if a snake is removed from its egg a little too early, it will writhe about, unable to move along properly, although in every other way it looks quite normal. It therefore seems likely that the snake only becomes fully co-ordinated just before hatching.

BIG BABIES
The young of the adder, Britain's only venomous snake, are incredibly large compared with the eggs in which they develop (pp. 20–21).

LOOKS CAN DECEIVE

Most geckos lay their eggs between pieces of bark or stuck to a wall. This sandstone gecko laid her eggs between the crevices of rocks, and because they were exposed to the elements, they had hard shells (pp. 20–21). Although many geckos lay their eggs in shared sites, they take no care of their young at all – in fact, it is unusual that mother and young should be as close to one another as this. The young are independent from birth, and are not sexually mature, that is able to reproduce, for about 18 months.

Female

Young

THE HAZARDS OF HATCHING

Among the reptiles, turtles lay the most eggs, but care for them the least. Abandoned to the earth or sand in which its egg was buried, from the start this little hatchling will have to fight alone to survive in a dangerous world.

The young snake checks its surroundings with its tongue

The snake is in no hurry to leave the safety of its shell

2 BREAKING THE SHELL

While it is developing inside the egg, the young rat snake takes nourishment from the yolk. A day or two before hatching, the yolk sac is drawn into the body and the remaining yolk is absorbed into the young snake's intestine. A small scar, rather like a tummy button, shows the point where the embryo was joined to its food supply. As the young snake develops, a sharp, but temporary "egg tooth" grows from the tip of its upper jaw and the hatchling uses this to pierce the egg shell. The young snake gets its first view of the world through one of the slits it makes.

3 LEAVING THE EGG

Having tested its surroundings by flicking its tongue in and out (pp. 16–17), the young snake cautiously leaves its shell. It will be in no hurry to leave, and may stay where it is, with only its head poking out, for a day or two. That way, if disturbed, it can always go back inside the egg. Rat snakes are usually finally ready to leave their eggs 7–15 weeks after laying.

5 MINOR MIRACLE

Fully out of its shell now, it seems amazing that such a long snake could ever have been packed inside such a relatively small egg. The hatchlings may be as much as seven times longer than the egg, 28–40 cm (11–16 in).

Scale tale

Reptiles have dry, scaly skins. As in other creatures, the skin forms a barrier between the animal's tissues and the world outside, protecting it from ordinary wear and tear, from drying out, and from damage by predators. The reptiles' scales are thickenings of this outside layer of skin, and are mostly made of a horny substance called keratin, rather like finger nails. The outer skin is shed from time to time and renewed by cells in the inner layer. This allows room for growth, and also replaces worn-out skin. Lizards and snakes have a special moulting, or "sloughing" time. Most lizards shed their skin in large flakes, often over a few days, while snakes slough the entire skin at one time.

Old skin is fragile and can break easily

Skin deep

Reptilian skin varies greatly from one species to another. It may be bumpy, or raised into defensive spines, as on the tails of certain lizards. Or it may form crests on the neck, back, or tail. In most snakes, the belly scales form a series of wide overlapping plates, which help the snakes when moving (pp. 52–53).

COUNTING THE SCALES
The pattern of scales on different parts of the head and body are valuable in helping specialists to identify reptiles. In snakes, for example, the number of scale rows at the mid-body line and the number of large belly scales are particularly helpful clues.

Caiman back

Smooth caiman belly skin

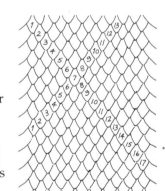

ON THE CREST
The scales of the skin of the chameleon rise to a crest of points running the length of its back.

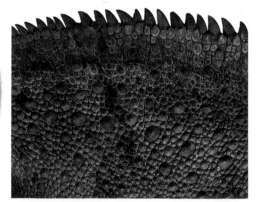

HORNY-SKINNED
The caiman's "armour" is made of rough horny scales, or scutes, along the back and tail. The back scales are strengthened by bony plates.

DIGGERS
The scales of skinks are smooth, so that mud does not cling to them.

PLATED LIZARD
Like the caiman, this lizard has bony plates under its scales.

New skin is smooth and shiny

RENEWING THE RATTLE

The tail of the rattlesnake is made up of a series of hollow pieces of keratin locked together. Every time the snake sheds its skin, a new segment is added to the rattle. To warn away its enemies, the snake shakes the rattle by vibrating its tail, and the separate pieces knock together to produce the rattle sound. It is a simple, but effective device.

SLOUGHING

About four times a year, the slow worm sheds its skin in very large pieces. Although it looks like a snake, it is in fact a legless lizard from Europe. Adult lizards moult about once every month when they are most active. Some lizards pull off their old skin with their mouth and swallow the strips, while the slow worm peels off its old skin, rather like a snake. The need to shed their skin continues throughout life, because most reptiles never stop growing, although the growth rate is almost undetectable when they are old.

SHARP DRESSING

When a cat sharpens its claws, it is also getting rid of dead tissue. People too, shed the dead, outer layer of their skin, although they only lose little pieces at a time! Humans also have to "shed" their clothes regularly as they grow up, rather as a snake needs a new, larger skin. Clothes offer protection from the world around us, as our skin is not as efficient as a reptile's.

ALL IN THE EYE

Several days before a snake is ready to shed its skin, its eyes look cloudy. Its skin appears dull and colourless, it loses its appetite, and may become aggressive. Many snakes also look for water, as they lose a considerable amount of body fluids along with their skins.

NEW SKIN FOR OLD

Snakes are able to crawl out of their old skin, usually leaving it behind in one piece. They can do this because they have no limbs which might hinder the shedding, and because their outer skin comes off as an all-in-one suit. The sloughing starts along the lips. The snake rubs the side of its head along the ground to turn the skin back; it then crawls out of its skin, turning it inside out as it does so. Often in no more than half an hour, the snake emerges, shining and glistening, in its new colours and scales.

Top

Adult rat snake skin

Young rat snake skin

Underside

Young snakes shed soon after they hatch and about seven times in their first year

Snake selection

Snakes have no legs, eyelids, or ear drums. Despite this, they have managed to survive very well, and frighten more people than any other creature. Their undeserved reputation is probably due to inherited fear of their strangeness, for although they kill 30 – 40,000 people every year, only about one tenth of them are dangerous to man. There are about 2,500 species of snakes, from thread snakes at 10 cm (4 in) to pythons at 10 m (32 ft).

BOTTOMS UP
When threatened, this harmless, long-nosed snake tries an effective, but nasty defensive trick; it hides its head under its coiled body, waves its tail in the air and shoots blood-stained liquid from its anal opening. It lives in prairies and deserts in the USA and Mexico and uses its pointed snout to burrow.

BACK BITER
This mildly venomous, rear-fanged Madagascan hognose snake rarely bites people. It is quite happy with its diet of small mammals and amphibians, but if it is threatened, it will flatten its neck (rather like a cobra) and hiss loudly. It shelters in burrows in grassland areas on the island of Madagascar, and grows up to 152 cm (5 ft) long.

NIGHT-TIME PROWLER
Another snake harmless to people, is the Californian mountain kingsnake. It is also one of the most attractive snakes found in North America. When it is warm, this snake takes life easy and hunts at night for lizards, other snakes and young birds. 102 cm (40 in) long, it is found from northern California to southern Washington state.

CHECKMATE
This non-poisonous, American snake is called the corn snake because the chequered markings on its underside look like the colour patterns on grains of Indian corn. The longest on record measured 183 cm (72 in).

SHRINKING VIOLET
This shy, grey-banded kingsnake is rarely seen in the wild. Despite its secretive habits this harmless snake is a popular pet and has bred successfully in captivity. 121 cm (47 in) when fully grown, it lives on a diet of lizards.

STONY LOOK
Medusa was a terrifying being. Her head was covered with writhing snakes and anyone unlucky enough to glance at her would turn instantly to stone.

BE GONE
Because Ireland
has no snakes,
legend says that St
Patrick banished
them to rid the
country of evil.

IN THE BEGINNING
Since the Garden of Eden,
when the devil in the form of a
serpent tempted Eve with fruit from
the forbidden tree, snakes have
never been very popular. This
painting of the
scene by
Albrecht
Dürer,
was
painted
in 1504.

STOCK STILL
The vine snake from south-east Asia spends hours motionless, hanging in the trees. Because it is bright green and very slender, it is well hidden. Its eyes face forwards, giving it binocular vision. As a result, it is good at judging distances, especially when lunging at passing lizards.

DOUBLE BLUFF
This harmless Sinaloan milk snake,
looks very like the highly venomous
coral snake. This happy chance may
deter quite a few predators
from trying to make a meal
of the snake. Milk snakes
are so-called because
of a mistaken belief
that they steal
milk from cows.

THE PITS
The copperhead is a North
American member of the pit
viper family. Like its relatives
the rattlesnakes, the
copperhead can inflict a nasty
bite. Its venom enters the
victim's bloodstream, causing
internal bleeding. However,
people rarely die from
copperhead bites.

Eye facing forwards

HIGH FLIER
The flying snake is an energetic, rapid-moving tree snake
from southern Asia. Active by day, it hangs high up in the
trees of thick forests, hunting for lizards and the occasional
frog. It jumps from branch to branch and even glides through
the air to lower levels. When it wants to slow down, it
flattens its body to increase air resistance.

Loads of lizards

THERE ARE OVER 3,000 SPECIES OF LIZARD. They form the most successful of all the reptilian groups, having evolved many different lifestyles. Although most of them live on the ground, many live in trees, some are burrowers, and still more are aquatic. Some lizards have no limbs and are rather snake-like. Others can parachute or fly. Geckos, iguanas, chameleons, skinks, and monitors are just a few of the lizards alive today.

MEEK AND MILD
In spite of its fierce appearance, the spiky moloch is harmless. It lives almost exclusively on ants. Apart from giving any predator a prickly mouthful, the moloch's spikes have another use. Dew condenses on them and runs into the lizard's mouth; it can then live for weeks without drinking.

PUNK IS ALIVE
The common iguana's crest, running like the teeth of a comb down the centre of its back, makes it easy to spot. These lizards are often seen basking in trees.

BLUE MOVER
The blue-tongued skink is so-called because of its blue tongue which it constantly flicks in and out. This skink gives birth to live young. It can move quite fast when necessary, despite its rather clumsy looks.

KOMODO KING
The Komodo dragon, a monitor lizard, is the largest living lizard in the world. One captured specimen was 3.10 m (10 ft 2 in) in length and weighed a staggering 165.6 kg (365 lb). The dragon is found only on a few Indonesian islands.

ARMOUR PLATED
Plated lizards have tough, bony plates underlying their scales. These lizards normally have long tails but this one has clearly had a narrow escape and its tail has not yet fully regrown (pp. 24–25).

FLAT AS A PANCAKE

This African lizard, like many of its family, has a flattened body and thick protective scales, so that it can slip easily into cracks in boulders. When threatened by a predator, it can jam itself into a crevice where it inflates its body, so that it is very difficult to prise out.

BLINKING GECKOS

Leopard geckos are unusual in that they have movable eyelids. Most geckos, like snakes, cannot blink, but have a fixed, transparent spectacle protecting their eyes. Their toes end in tiny, strong adhesive pads which can cling to smooth surfaces.

COLOUR CONSCIOUS

Chameleons lead generally calm lives, which is fortunate, as apart from their ability to change colour, they have little defence against enemies. The male Jackson's chameleon is better off than most – his prehistoric-looking, three-pronged horns would frighten away a good many foes.

TREE CREEPER

The glossy-skinned, emerald tree skink rarely ventures onto the ground, but spends most of its life scuttling amid the branches of trees in Indonesia.

Emerald tree skink

A TOE TO TAIL TALE

Chameleons have truly remarkable toes specialized for life in trees. The toes are so arranged that the feet are able to clasp branches securely, while the tail offers extra support, twisting and twining itself around any handy twig. This Madagascan chameleon, like many others, also boasts a strange tongue. Sticky tipped, it can be rapidly shot out further than the length of its body, guaranteeing it a good diet of insects and other small invertebrates.

GOOD INFLUENCE

In Chinese art, the common lizard has evolved into a magnificent dragon. The dragon in Chinese folklore is the symbol of rebirth and fertility. Because it is thought to be a gentle creature dispersing happiness, it plays a large part in the famous street festivals of many Chinese communities.

Strong tail used for securing posture and for balance

EYED LIZARD

The eyed or ocellated lizard is only found in Europe and North Africa. It is one of Europe's largest lizards, sometimes growing to a length of 80 cm (2 ft 7 in). This shy lizard is really a ground dweller but can climb well.

Turtles and tortoises

TURTLE GOD
In Brahmin mythology, after one of the great floods, the god Vishnu returned to earth as the turtle Kurma. He came to help rescue the world.

REPTILES WITH SHELLS (chelonians) are found in most warm and hot parts of the world. There are between 250 and 300 species, and the shell protects the reptile from knocks and bumps, poor weather conditions, and predators. It is also good camouflage. Chelonians live in salt water, fresh water, and on land. Marine chelonians are called turtles and the rest are tortoises, but sometimes pond and river dwellers are known as terrapins. All chelonians lay eggs on land in a variety of different habitats. Some lay in sand, some in leaf litter and some in the burrows of other animals. The number of eggs laid varies with the body size of the mother. The smaller species lay one to four eggs per clutch, whereas some large sea turtles regularly lay over 100 eggs at a time.

GALAPAGOS GIANTS
Charles Darwin wrote about the Galapagos Islands in the Pacific Ocean in 1835. He found the giant tortoises had adapted to life on their own island. There are two main groups: the saddlebacks, which reach up to tall vegetation for their food, and the domeshells which graze on the ground.

LONESOME GEORGE
On the island of Santa Cruz in the Galapagos Islands, a giant tortoise, nearly 1 m (3 ft) in length, lives alone. He appears to be the last remaining giant tortoise from the neighbouring Pinta Island. Many attempts have been made to find a female from the same island, but without success. It seems George will live and die alone.

HALF AND HALF
Pond terrapins are mainly vegetarian and spend most of their time in water, although they do come on to land to bask. The lungs of some of the pond terrapins of southern Asia are enclosed in bony boxes formed by the inner walls of the shell. This is to protect the lungs from increased pressure when the animals dive deeply. The European pond terrapin is found throughout Europe, western Asia, and north west Africa. It is a shy creature and dives into the water when approached.

The carapace covers the back

The plastron covers the belly

Shell is made up of 59 to 61 bones, and is in two parts, the plastron and the carapace

RED EARS
Red-eared terrapins get their names because of the broad, red stripe that runs along the side of the head. Because they are gentle and attractive creatures they are very popular as pets. Unfortunately, they seldom reach maturity in captivity because they do not receive the vitamins and minerals they need. Found in the United States, they live in ponds and rivers, but frequently climb out of the water to bask, often on logs where they may pile up several deep.

The red or yellow "ear marking" makes this turtle instantly recognizable

The plastron and carapace are joined on each side by a girdle bone

LETHAL SOFTY
The shell of soft-shelled turtles has no horny plates and feels like leather. In Africa, Asia, Indonesia, and North America they are usually to be found buried in mud in rivers and ponds, although like many turtles they enjoy basking in the sun. They are able to breathe in water, by stretching their long necks to the surface and taking a breath through the snorkel-like nose. They hide from enemies, but are fierce and effective hunters and can strike at lightning speed.

RECORD REPTILE
The leatherback is the largest of all living turtles and, according to some records, it is also the heaviest. In 1988, this enormous leatherback drowned when it became entangled in fishermen's line. It was washed up in Harlech Bay in Wales. Weighing 752 kg (2016 lb), it was the biggest turtle ever recorded. These turtles breed in the Caribbean, then follow jellyfish, their main food, across the Atlantic.

Hawksbill turtle shell

Large scales, called scutes, cover the bone of the shell

Starred tortoise shell

Radiated tortoise shell

SHELLS
Different life-styles lead to alterations in shell structure. Land tortoises usually have high-domed or knobbly shells as a defence against a predator's strong jaws. Turtles tend to have flatter shells, which are streamlined for easy movement through the water. The soft-shelled turtles have the flattest shells, to allow them to hide easily beneath sand and mud.

Turtle tank

IN FOLKLORE, THE ALLIGATOR SNAPPING TURTLE was thought to be a cross between a common turtle and an alligator. It is well-named and is ferocious both in appearance and in its habits. Its head is so powerful that it can do considerable damage to a person's fingers or toes with its knife-like jaws. It spends nearly all its time in water. When fishing for prey, the animal lies motionless on the river bed, its mouth wide open. It will eat practically anything that it can catch, including snails and clams and even other turtles. Any object too large to swallow in one piece, is simply chopped in half by the jaws. It is one of the largest freshwater turtles in the world and can grow to 66 cm (26 in) and weigh up to 91 kg (200 lb).

Worm-like appendage

Sharp jaws used to cut prey

WIGGLY WORM
One of the most remarkable features of the alligator snapper is the worm-like appendage on the end of its tongue. This fills with blood which colours it red and it then resembles an earthworm on a fishing hook. It has a wide "tail" end and a narrower "head" end. When hungry, the turtle lies very still on the bottom of the river, opens its mouth and wiggles the "worm". Unwary passing prey are tempted to grab the bait, and the jaws of the turtle snap shut.

Turtle rises on its forelegs when faced with an aggressor

SUCKED TO DEATH

The weird-looking matamata turtle from South America, like the alligator snapper, also lies on the bottom of rivers waiting for prey, and it also has a strange method of catching it. When prey approaches, the matamata expands its throat. This creates a strong enough current to suck the unsuspecting prey into its jaws.

Ridged and roughened shell provides both protection and camouflage

Very powerful forelegs often used to hold prey

UNSAFE TO BATHE

The alligator snapper looks very much like a stone, especially when its ridged shell is covered with algae. It relies on this superb camouflage to trap its prey. Careless bathers in this river in the USA could have toes severely damaged by the blade-like jaws.

The crocodile clan

CROCODILES, along with their relatives the alligators, caimans, and gharials, are ancient animals. They belong to the same group of creatures that included the dinosaurs and the ancestors of the birds. The crocodile family spends a lot of time basking or lying in water. But when necessary they can move tremendously fast, attacking with immense power and precision. Despite their ferocity, crocodile parents take care of their young more than any other group of living reptiles. The same smiling jaws that can kill an animal as huge as a wildebeest can carry and protect babies only a few centimetres long.

CROCODILE GOD
Sobek, the crocodile god of ancient Egypt, gradually developed from a minor protective god to one of the most important of all the Egyptian deities. No one knows whether he became a god because he was so feared.

Gharial skull
(top view)

EGYPTIAN MUMMIES
In ancient Egypt many animals, including the crocodile, were sacred. In some of the temples, crocodiles were looked after in special pools, draped with pendants of gold and precious stones. When they died they were embalmed, or mummified.

A STITCH IN TIME
Mary Queen of Scots was held as a prisoner by Queen Elizabeth I from 1569 – 1584. She and her gaoler set to work embroidering this massive wall hanging. The crocodile is just one of the many animals they produced. Presumably the work had a calming effect on Mary as she awaited her execution.

GHARIAL
Strangest of all the crocodiles, the gharial has a long narrow snout with rather small, piercing teeth. The snout sweeps through the water, while the interlocking and outwardly pointing teeth are perfect for grasping slippery fish. The adult male wards off rivals by a loud buzz made through the knob, or ghara, on its nose. The noise is produced as the gharial breathes out – useful as its jaws are not particularly powerful.

Gharial skull
(side view)

Caiman

Caiman skull
(side view)

Caiman skull
(top view)

CAIMAN
Caimans are members of the alligator family. Their snouts are rather short and broad and, as with alligators, the teeth on the lower jaw are largely invisible when the mouth is closed. Young caimans eat mainly insects, but as they grow their diet includes water snails, fish, mammals, and birds. One species of broad-snouted caiman is particularly adaptable and has been seen in cattle ponds and near large cities in heavily polluted rivers.

Crocodile skull
(side view)

Eye sockets

Prominent tooth

Crocodile skull
(top view)

CROCODILE
In crocodiles some of the teeth on the lower jaw stick out above the upper jaw when the mouth is shut. They are perfect for gripping and punching, but are not so good at slicing and chewing. When a crocodile is eating an animal as large as a buffalo, it will seize part of the carcass in its jaws, and roll over and over, until a chunk is torn away.

Alligator skull
(side view)

Lower jaw
opening

ALLIGATOR
Despite looking very clumsy, the American alligator can use its jaws with surprising delicacy. The female, for example, sometimes helps her eggs to hatch by lifting them into her mouth. She gently cracks them open by rolling them against the roof of her mouth with her tongue. This is a massive creature, reaching up to 6 m (20 ft) in length.

Alligator skull
(top view)

External
nostrils

The living fossil

THE TUATARA IS A "LIVING FOSSIL", so-called because it is the sole survivor of a group of animals that is extinct, and is only otherwise found preserved, or fossilized, in rocks. In fact, it is remarkable that the tuatara has survived, and no-one really knows why, because its closest relatives died out millions of years ago. Today, tuataras live on a few small islands off the coast of New Zealand, where they are active at night. They inhabit burrows which are also often occupied by seabirds (pp. 60–61). Although the tuatara looks very like a lizard, it differs from lizards in a number of ways. Tuataras have a low metabolic rate (the rate of conversion of food into energy), and are able to function well in much colder temperatures than other reptiles. They also have an extremely slow growth rate and are sometimes still growing at 50–60 years of age.

Male

Female

KITH OR KIN?
These are the fossilized remains of *Homoeosaurus*, a tuatara-like animal that lived about 140 million years ago in what is now Europe. "Sphenodontida", the group that contains the tuatara and its fossil relatives, were very widespread and successful animals at that time. It seems likely that the sphenodontids separated from early lizards some 200 million years ago.

Short, strong legs suitable for excavating burrows

Tuatara, the Maori word meaning "peaks on the back", refers to the crest which runs down the back and tail

RESURRECTION

Another true living fossil is the coelacanth, which means "hollow spine". It was the name given to a group of fish which lived from 300 to 90 million years ago. After this time, they were thought to be extinct and were known only as fossils. However, in 1938, a live coelacanth was caught off the coast of South Africa and there were hopes that other coelacanths might live in the region. But it was not until 14 years later, that the coelacanth "home" was discovered in deep waters off the coast of the Comoro Islands, northwest of Madagascar.

GROWING OLD TOGETHER

Male tuataras grow to a length of about 61 cm (2ft), but females are slightly shorter. They reach sexual maturity at about 20 years of age and can possibly live to more than 120. They have no external ear openings, and the male has no sexual organ. After mating the female stores the sperm for 10–12 months and then lays 5–15 eggs in a shallow burrow. The eggs do not hatch for another 15 months, the longest incubation period of any reptile, and the young are self-sufficient immediately after birth.

A third "eye" is sensitive to light. Visible in the young animal, the skin thickens over this organ in the adult. It may regulate the "biological clock" of the tuatara and also possibly acts as a thermostat

Teeth are part of the jaw bone which has serrated edges

Bony arches

SKULL STRUCTURE

The tuatara's skull differs from that of lizards in that two bony arches frame the back, rather like a crocodilian's. In most lizards, the lower arch is missing, while in snakes and many burrowing lizards, both arches have gone.

Duck-billed platypus

Echidna (spiny anteater)

ODD MEN OUT

Although the duck-billed platypus and the spiny echidna are not strictly "living fossils", they are certainly primitive and very unusual mammals. The platypus has the bill of a duck and the tail of a beaver, and the spiny anteater bears a strong resemblance to a hedgehog. Like reptiles, both these mammals are egg layers.

A bite to eat

MOST REPTILES ARE MEAT EATERS. Crocodiles and snakes are all carnivores, and have perfected methods of eating their food, but some snakes have specialized diets, including birds' eggs (pp. 44–45), and fish eggs (eaten by some sea snakes). Many of the lizards are also predators, feeding on insects, mammals, birds, and other reptiles. The Komodo dragon has serrated teeth rather like a shark's, which it uses to cut chunks of flesh from prey as big as water buffalos. Among the lizards, however, large iguanas, some of the bigger skinks, and a few agamids are mostly vegetarian. Tortoises eat a wide variety of plants, but even they occasionally eat meat. Freshwater turtles often eat worms, snails, fish, and other small animals. Sea turtles generally feed on jellyfish, crabs, molluscs, and fish, but they also eat plants. In fact, the green turtle eats little except sea grass.

SLOW BUT SURE
Very few tortoises or turtles have the speed or agility to catch fast-moving prey. As a result, most feed on vegetation, or on slow-moving animals, such as molluscs, worms, and insect larvae. They all make the most of food that is nearby. As well as fleshy plants, the spur-thighed tortoise also enjoys the occasional morsel of any dead animal it finds.

HOOK MEETS HIS END
In J.M. Barrie's *Peter Pan*, Hook is haunted by the crocodile who has already eaten his hand – and is looking for more! Helped for a time by a clock that ticks in the creature's stomach, Hook is finally tricked.

CROCODILE LARDER
Nile crocodiles occasionally share the carcass of a large animal such as a wildebeest or a buffalo. Crocodile stomachs are only the size of a basketball, so crocodiles cannot eat a big animal all at once. Prey is often, therefore, left in one spot to be finished off later. This has led to the mistaken belief that crocodiles like to eat rotten meat, hiding a freshly killed animal until it is "high". In fact, they prefer fresh meat.

Armlets

Pieces of turtle shell

Stones

Bangle

Porcupine quills

STOMACH STORE
Crocodiles often devour hard, heavy objects, such as stones and pieces of metal. One can only hope that no-one was wearing the bangle when it was swallowed! The objects may be eaten to help the crocodile to digest its food.

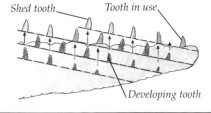

Shed tooth *Tooth in use*

Developing tooth

DEVELOPING TEETH
Mammals have two sets of teeth – baby, or "milk" teeth and then an adult set. Crocodiles, on the other hand, shed their teeth throughout their lives, with new ones constantly replacing the old ones. The developing teeth grow up through the holes of those already in use.

Eyed lizards are mainly ground-dwellers, but are also excellent climbers. Crickets and grasshoppers are their favourite food

CRISPY CRICKET

After a rapid chase, the eyed lizard grabs a cricket with its jaws, and shakes its victim violently to stun it. It passes the cricket to the back of its mouth, its jaws moving over the prey in a succession of snapping movements. The lizard's teeth grip and release the cricket as the jaws are raised and lowered. It is important that the lizard moves fast – the cricket may not yet be totally stunned and will not waste an opportunity to try and escape. The majority of lizards are insect eaters and in some areas are important in keeping insect populations down.

SHARPSHOOTERS

With tongues as long as their bodies and tails, chameleons have been described as the sharpshooters of the lizards. The tongue is hollow and unforked with a large, sticky tip, and can be shot from the mouth by a contracting muscle at lightning speed and with tremendous accuracy. A second set of muscles is used to draw the tongue back into the mouth, where it is kept bunched up until it is needed again.

A tight squeeze

ALL SNAKES EAT MEAT. There are no vegetarians, and snakes have had to develop many different ways of killing their food. Some kill their prey with venom (pp. 42–43), but boas and pythons feed mainly on mammals, which they kill by constriction. Constrictors do not crush their victims as many people think. The snake coils its body around its struggling victim, making it harder and harder for the prey to breathe, until it finally suffocates. The snake applies just enough pressure to match the breathing movements of its prey. Any mammal from a mouse to a deer is chosen, depending on the size of the snake. In fact the giant snakes can swallow surprisingly big animals. An anaconda over 8 m (25 ft) long can eat a caiman nearly 2 m (6 ft) long, although it may take more than a week to digest.

TINTIN TO THE RESCUE!
There are a few Asian and African records of humans who have been killed and eaten by some of the larger species of pythons. In one of the well-known *Tintin* books, Zorrino the guide has a lucky escape (contrary to appearances here), saved just in time by his friend Tintin.

DANGEROUS ACT
Music hall and circus act performers who dance with constrictors, are taking a great risk. This dancer was nearly suffocated by a python – and was rescued only seconds before certain death.

2 DEADLY EMBRACE
The constricting snake reacts to every minute movement of the rat, tightening its grip all the time. It responds to even the smallest vibrations produced by the rat's beating heart, and the snake will not release its hold until the beating finally stops. Death is fairly quick and bones are rarely broken. The snake shifts the rat into a good position so that it can be swallowed head first. That way it slips down the throat quite easily.

3 BIG MOUTH
The snake's mouth is very flexible. The jaws move easily, with the upper and lower jaws moving from side to side, while the backward-pointing teeth grip tightly. As the powerful jaws move over the head of the rat, it looks as though the snake is "walking over" its food.

4 SAFETY FIRST
It may take only one or two gulps before a small animal disappears completely, but it takes an hour or more for some of the larger victims. The swallowing action of the snake is mainly automatic, as the prey is drawn in by the trunk muscles of the snake. If, however, the snake is frightened or disturbed while it is eating it is able to regurgitate its meal in order to escape.

Body can expand to allow for large prey

5 TIGHT FIT
Now, most of the rat has disappeared. The flexible ligament, rather like an elastic muscle that connects the two halves of the snake's lower jaw, allows the snake to open its mouth very wide. As the lower jaws are forced apart, the muscle between them stretches to the shape of the prey.

DINNER TIME

If a meal walks by that might put up a dangerous fight, a snake can usually afford to ignore it. After an enormous feast, when a constrictor might work its way through an entire leopard, the snake may not eat again for as much as a year.

1 FANGS OF DEATH

When a hungry boa constrictor attacks its prey, its problem is to find an end where it can start swallowing. This is usually the head end. If the victim is wriggly and fat, like this rat, the snake will strike with its long front teeth. Having secured the rat in its jaws, the snake starts to coil round it.

Prey is swallowed headfirst so that it cannot attack the snake

Jaw closed

Jaw open

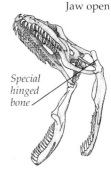

Special hinged bone

OPEN WIDE

The jaws of a snake are very flexible, so prey can be swallowed headfirst and whole, even when the victim's body is wider than the snake's. A special bone, linking the lower jaw to the skull, works like a double-jointed hinge. The lower jaw can be stretched sideways, because the two halves are connected at the chin by a flexible ligament that works like an elastic muscle.

SNAKE EATS SNAKE

When a Californian king snake meets a rattlesnake, it grips the rattler with its jaws just behind the head. Then the king snake loops its body around the victim, squeezing until the rattler suffocates.

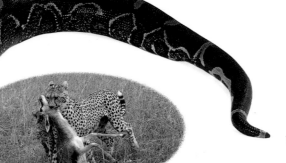

WILD CAT STRIKE

In Kenya, a Thompson's gazelle falls victim to a cheetah. The massive jaws of the cat clamp on to the throat of the struggling prey, probably causing it to suffocate – in the same way as a boa suffocates its prey. But no-one really knows whether the gazelle dies by strangulation, or whether it is finished off by the sharp, pointed teeth and powerful claws of the cheetah.

6 THE END OF THE ROAD

At this point the snake could face breathing problems, but it overcomes the problem by pushing its windpipe forward towards the front of its mouth, using it as a built-in "snorkel".

Name your poison

THE ONLY POISONOUS, or venomous reptiles, apart from two lizards, are snakes. Poisonous snakes are found in many parts of the world in most habitats, but the most venomous species tend to be concentrated in tropical areas. A snake injects poison, or venom, into its prey, using specially adapted teeth or fangs. In the most dangerous venomous snakes, like vipers, cobras, and sea snakes, the fangs are found at the front of the upper jaw, but in other snakes they can be positioned at the back. The venom itself is a complicated cocktail which affects the prey's nervous system, tissues, or blood – or all three. Its main purpose is to subdue the prey so that the snake can then kill it, but it is also sometimes used for defence. Most snakes, however, will try to avoid a fight, escaping when possible.

Cheek muscles contract, forcing venom out

CRUEL TO BE KIND
Milking snakes for their venom is still practised in many parts of the world, as venom is used to produce serum (fluid used in medicines to prevent the action of poison) against snake bites. The snake is held by the back of the head and made to bite through tissue covering the top of a small container. It is then forced to eject the venom by gentle pressure on the venom sac in the cheeks. In time, the animal produces more venom.

RATTLESNAKE
Rattlesnakes are extremely venomous snakes. They are sometimes known as pit vipers, because they have a remarkably keen, heat-sensitive pit between their nostrils and eyes to enable them to locate prey at night. Even in total darkness, they can detect and strike accurately at objects only a fraction of a degree warmer than their surroundings. The belief that a rattlesnake's age can be determined by the number of rattles on its tail is untrue. In fact, the snake may shed its skin and add a new rattle two or three times a year.

Sea snake

Gila monster

OTHER POISONERS
The sea snake is the most venomous snake in the world. It can also swim extremely fast and stay under water for up to five hours. There are two species of poisonous lizard – the Gila monster and the Mexican beaded lizard. Both are found in the south western USA and parts of Mexico. Their venom comes from saliva glands in the lower jaw, and the lizards chew it into the victim.

Venom passes through tube

Hole in the tip of the fang

Venom sac

FANG FACTS
The fangs of a rattlesnake are folded back against the roof of the mouth until needed, when they are swung forward into position. A pair are used at a time, with one or more spare pairs arranged in formation behind them.

SOLO SHREW
The short-tailed shrew is the only mammal with a venomous bite. It has glands in its mouth that produce a nerve poison. When this little creature bites its prey, usually smaller mammals, the venom in the saliva enters the wound and is powerful enough to kill in seconds.

STAR PERFORMERS

Snakes have featured in literature for hundreds of years. In Shakespeare's *Antony and Cleopatra*, Cleopatra committed suicide using an asp, generally thought to be the cobra commonly found in Egypt and East Africa. Its bite can be deadly from the moment the snake leaves the shell. Sometimes, snakes also star in films, such as *True Grit*. Here, John Wayne examines Kim Darby's hand after she has been bitten.

Antony and Cleopatra.
Act 5 No.2.

SNAKE STONES

Snake stones were once wrongly thought to cure snake bites. They were often made of burnt bone, chalk, horn, or other absorbent materials, which were believed to "absorb" the venom from a bite when pressed against it.

Special scales make up rattle

Hollow segments which lock together

Rattle

Rapid vibration produces a sizzling sound

Egg-eating snakes

THE PROBLEM OF CATCHING live food is solved if prey is caught young enough. Some snakes eat nothing but eggs and have become particularly specialized for the task. Small eggs, especially the soft-shelled ones laid by lizards and some other snakes, are easy to eat, as they can be quickly slit open by the snake's teeth. Larger, hard-shelled eggs, such as those laid by birds, need special treatment. True egg-eating snakes eat only birds' eggs, which they swallow whole as they have few teeth. Instead they have tooth-like spines that stick out from the backbone and crack open the egg as it passes down to the snake's throat.

Diet of eggs

One problem with an egg diet is that food is not always available. In some parts of the world, birds only lay their eggs at certain times of the year, and so a snake may have to go for a long time without food. Fortunately, egg-eating snakes can bring up or regurgitate, egg shell. This means that no space is wasted in the snake's stomach, and it can eat as many eggs as it finds. Nor does the snake waste vital energy in passing the shell through its digestive system.

2 SWALLOW HARD
The egg is passing down the snake's throat. The skin on the side of the neck is very elastic, and at this stage the egg is still unbroken.

Head arched down, pushing egg against bony inner spines to puncture shell

Finely interlinked scales separate as skin stretches

3 SPINY BONES
The passage of the egg has now been stopped by the tooth-like spines on the underside of the neck bones.

A valve at the entrance to the stomach accepts yolks and liquids, but rejects pieces of shell

The "bulge" is noticeably smaller

4 GOING DOWN...
Once the egg is punctured, the muscles of the snake's body work in waves to squeeze out the contents, which then continue on to the stomach. The snake now bends its body into S-shaped curves, forcing the collapsed shell back towards the mouth.

5 AND UP IT COMES
It may take from five minutes to an hour, depending on the size of the egg, for it to be completely swallowed. Finally, the snake gapes widely and the compacted cigar-shaped shell is brought up. The fragments of shell are still held together by the sticky egg membranes.

The jagged edges of the shell pieces are stuck together. All the goodness in the egg has been drained

Regurgitated shell

1 TOO GREEDY?

An African egg-eater is about to swallow an egg. It looks impossible – the egg is twice the width of the snake's body. It has a lightly-built skull and the mouth is lined with sticky ridges.

Mouth ridges grip the egg as it passes towards the snake's throat

Because of its shape, an egg is remarkably resistant to crushing before it is pierced by the snake's bony spines

STOP! THIEF!

The monitor lizards, which include some of the giants of the reptilian world, are well-known for their greed. Many live on the carcasses of dead animals and on live animals - but even a nest of eggs is not safe with them around.

Survival

REPTILES USE A VARIETY OF METHODS to frighten away their enemies. Some can camouflage themselves (pp. 48–49) to avoid being seen in the first place. Others may scare predators by inflating themselves with air, then blowing it out with a loud hiss. Several lizards and some snakes try to protect their vulnerable head and trunk by sacrificing their tail. Some American horned lizards swell up in defence, and at the same time squirt blood from tiny capillaries in the eyes. It is possible that the blood irritates other animals' eyes. The armadillo lizard from South Africa protects its soft-skinned belly by coiling itself up into a tight ball. Although it cannot escape by rolling away in this position, its thick, spiny scales running the length of its head, back, and tail, create a perfect shield.

ON GUARD

One of the most spectacular displays of any reptile is that of the Australian frilled lizard. The "frill" is a large flap of loose skin that is attached to the neck and is normally kept folded flat. When startled by a predator, the lizard erects this ruff-like collar, so that it is often more than four times the width of its body. If challenged, the lizard will also start to bob its head, lash its tail, and wave its legs about. While most lizards under attack will normally try to escape, the frilled lizard meets danger head on if predators get too close for comfort.

Gaping mouth expands the neck frill. The wider the mouth is opened, the more erect the frill becomes

STINKY STINKPOT

The skunk is a mammal that is well-known for the foul smell it produces when frightened or threatened. The stinkpot from the USA is a turtle that is just as evil-smelling, as its name suggests. The smell is produced by a pair of glands in the soft skin of the turtle's thighs. Apart from being very smelly when frightened, it is also aggressive, so it is unlikely to be set upon by too many predators.

Frill fully erected to scare aggressors

Tail is lashed back and forth

Stinkpot

Skunk

Extended claws and flexed feet provide strong balance

SURVIVAL KIT

If people are to survive in adverse conditions, they have to take special clothes and equipment. Although reptiles cannot survive extreme temperatures, they can adapt to changing weather conditions within their own environment.

THE TALE OF A TAIL

When grabbed by the tail, most lizards will shed it. Although a dramatic method of defence, loss of a tail is better than certain death. Several lizards waggle their tail when first attacked and this helps to confuse the attacking animal. The vertebrae, or small back bones, along the tail have special cracks marking the spots where it can break off. When the tail is grasped, the muscles, which are also arranged so that they will separate neatly, contract. This causes one of the vertebrae to break off.

Fracture points along the tail

1 BREAKING FREE

This tree skink has lost part of its tail while breaking free from a predator. The shed part of the tail often twitches for several minutes after it has been severed, confusing the enemy for long enough for the lizard to escape.

Tail has been recently shed

Although the new tail looks the same on the outside, it has a simple tube of cartilage instead of vertebrae on the inside

2 GROWING STRONGER

In two months the tail has noticeably grown back. Losing it was quite costly, however. The lizard may have been storing food in it for a time when there might be little or none around, such as in winter or during a dry season. Some species are also known to live longer when they have a complete tail.

3 NEW FOR OLD

After eight months the tail has almost grown to its original full length. If necessary, the tail can be broken off again, but it will only be able to break in the old part, where there are still vertebrae and "cracking points".

Growing a new tail uses up a lot of energy that could have been put to better use

PLAYING DEAD

When all else fails, some snakes will pretend to be dead. When this European grass snake first meets an enemy it will puff and hiss loudly. If this does not work, the snake will roll over onto its back, wriggle (as though in the last stages of death) and then lie quite still, with its mouth wide open and its tongue hanging out. Although pretending to be dead may fool some animals, if the snake is turned over, it will repeat the trick, rather giving the game away!

Blending in

MANY REPTILES ARE ABLE TO CHANGE their appearance in order to make themselves hard to see against their natural background. This ability, known as camouflage, is used to avoid being spotted by enemies, but it is also used to help the reptile ambush unsuspecting prey. Some reptiles are naturally camouflaged, and their skin colours match their backgrounds perfectly. In others, the pattern on the skin helps to break up the outline of the body, and in a few, it is the shape of the animal that helps to improve this effect. The fleshy side fringes and leaf-shaped tails of the tree-living geckos, for example, help them to blend almost perfectly with the bark and lichen of the tree trunks they cling to.

COLOUR CONSCIOUS
Lizards, especially chameleons, are the true masters of camouflage. Many can make the colour of their skins lighter or darker as needed. Although these changes take place so that the chameleon can match its background, many other things influence the colour change. Light level, temperature, and the mood of the lizard (for example if it is frightened) can all affect the colour it takes on.

The chameleon's skin has several layers of colour cells. Beneath these are the melanophores, cells with tentacle-like arms that extend through the other layers.

The colour change is caused by the melanophores moving a dark brown pigment in and out of the upper layers of the skin

LEAF GREEN
Hard to spot against the palm trees on which they are commonly found, these little tree skinks live in the forests of Indonesia, the Philippines, and the Solomon Islands. The bright green and mottled brown of their bodies, make them almost invisible. Green is understandably a popular colour among tree-living reptiles active in the day.

FLOWER POWER
Do not be fooled by this little head. Beneath the leafy canopy is the large body of the Murray River turtle from eastern Australia. A powerful swimmer, it is mainly carnivorous, although it will eat a few plants.

48

DOUBLE TROUBLE

Lying still in the leaf litter of the forests of tropical Africa, these gaboon vipers are nearly invisible in the dappled light and shade, as they wait for rodents, frogs, and birds. Yet when one of the snakes is removed from its natural background, its vivid markings become strikingly obvious. Many people have compared the colourful geometrical skin patterns to those on oriental carpets. Although unaggressive and unlikely to attack, its bite would be dangerously venomous to anyone unfortunate enough to tread on one! In fact, the fangs of the gaboon viper are the longest of any snake, up to 50 mm (2 in) in a 1.80 m (6 ft) specimen.

Gaboon viper

HIDDEN DEPTHS

Luckily for this black caiman, it could be mistaken for rocks as it lies in the muddy waters. It is hunted for its skin and is constantly threatened. But its ability to lie unseen helps it when it is looking for food.

Lots of legs

Legs and feet play a vital part in the lives of many reptiles, although snakes and some lizards do very well with no limbs at all. Legs and feet are generally adapted to the habitat in which the reptile lives. Desert lizards, for example, often have long scales fringing their toes, which help them to walk on soft sand. Climbing lizards tend to have very sharp claws which allow them to grip, even smooth surfaces, firmly. Some climbing lizards, such as geckos, have adhesive pads as well. Webbed feet, or paddle-shaped limbs are found on some aquatic turtles. In other swimming reptiles, such as crocodiles and monitor lizards, the tail provides most of the propulsion and the limbs are folded back out of the way.

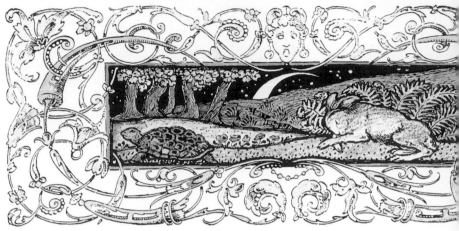

THE HARE AND THE TORTOISE
In the famous Aesop fable, the hare is so confident of winning his race with the slow and ponderous tortoise, that he falls asleep by the wayside and the tortoise crosses the finishing line first. It is certainly true that although tortoises are slow, they make steady progress and can travel quite long distances, seldom stopping for a rest.

LEGS ALLSORTS
The feet of a reptile very accurately reflect its lifestyle. The powerful feet and legs of lizards such as the monitors and the plated lizards, are good for digging. The sharp-clawed toes of the girdled lizards give the animals a grip when climbing, often on flaking rock surfaces. The slightly webbed back feet of the crocodilians help propel them through the water. In some of the smaller skinks, the limbs are so small that they barely support the animal.

Caiman

Plated lizard

All five toes spread out to achieve maximum grip

Monitor lizard

African girdled lizard

Blue-tongued skink

50

Geckos have no trouble moving vertically or hanging horizontally

GET A GRIP
The tokay is a fairly large gecko from east Asia. It is so-called because one of the noises it makes sounds very like "tokay". It is one of the best lizard climbers and has no difficulty scaling a wall, running across a ceiling, and even clinging to a sheet of glass. It grips by using pads on the underside of its fingers and toes. The pads are covered by microscopic, hair-like structures, which allows the gecko to cling to almost any surface. There may be as many as a million "hairs" on a tokay's pads, which rub the surface on which the animal is walking.

Elongated body resembles that of a snake

LOSS OF LEGS
This little glass lizard is often mistaken for a snake. It has no front legs, and only tiny, hardly visible, remnants of back legs. Many other lizards, particularly burrowing types, have evolved in the same way. Loss of legs is usually accompanied by lengthening of the body, which is therefore better equipped for a life underground. However, some legless lizards, like the glass lizard, live in rocky habitats or coiled in thick vegetation.

Vestigial limbs (small remnants of hind legs) are of no use in movement, but the male may use them in courtship to stimulate the female

LITTLE LIMBS
In most snakes, all traces of limbs have been lost. However, some of the more primitive groups, such as boas and pythons, have tiny remnants of the hip bones and hind limbs. The only external signs of these are small "claws" at the base of the tail, on either side of the vent.

Tokay gecko climbing

Ground control

MOST LIZARDS RELY ON SWIFTNESS and agility to hunt and get out of trouble. They usually use all four limbs and can move at speed. Their legs and feet are specially adapted to where they live. Turtles have no need for speed. Instead, they have powerful legs which can carry the extra weight of a protective shell and propel them forward slowly but surely. In spite of being without legs, snakes also move efficiently on land in a variety of ways. Their method of movement may change depending on their surroundings. Crocodilians are most at home in water, but when on land they usually crawl forwards, dragging their bellies along the ground. Occasionally, smaller crocodiles can perform a "gallop".

Palm flexed against the ground

Back legs provide most of the thrust

Tegu lizard

3 TWO AT A TIME
When a lizard breaks into a trot, the body is supported by two legs at a time (the diagonal pairs). There may even be times when both front feet and one hind foot are off the ground.

Long tail is used for balance

TWO LEGS ARE BETTER THAN FOUR
This crested water dragon comes from Asia and lives mainly in trees growing near water. If disturbed when on the ground, it may rear up on its hind legs and run along upright for short bursts, its tail helping it to balance. This type of bipedal (two-legged) locomotion occurs also in several other lizards. These lizards can achieve greater speed running on two legs than they can on four.

Alerted crested water dragon standing on all four paws

Lizard locomotion

Most lizards have four legs with five toes each, although there are some completely legless lizards and some with only tiny hind limbs. In most lizards, the back legs are stronger than the front and "power" the animal forward. Lizards which live underground often have much smaller legs or even none at all, as they tend to glide and wind through burrows, rather like snakes.

1 PALM POWER
When it is moving, the hand of this tegu lizard points forwards with the palm downwards, and much of the thrust comes from the palm being flexed against the ground.

2 SIDE TO SIDE
When the lizard is going fast, it increases its stride by bending its body from side to side. The order in which the limbs are moved depends on how fast the lizard is travelling. When walking slowly, three feet are kept on the ground at all times.

Snake movement

Snakes use four main methods of getting around without legs; serpentine motion, concertina motion, sidewinding, and rectilinear motion.

NOW YOU SEE ME...!
A sidewinding Namib desert adder has been here. The snake lifts loops of its body clear of the surface as it moves sideways, leaving these distinctive bar-like tracks. This method of movement stops the snake slipping when it is edging its way across a soft sand dune.

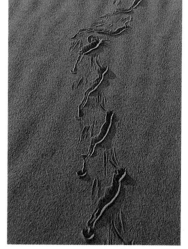

Sidewinding

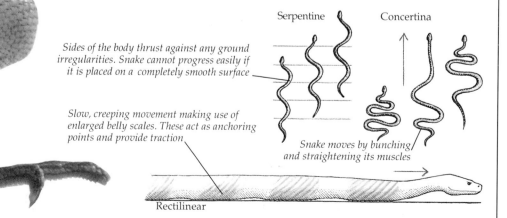

Serpentine Concertina

Sides of the body thrust against any ground irregularities. Snake cannot progress easily if it is placed on a completely smooth surface

Slow, creeping movement making use of enlarged belly scales. These act as anchoring points and provide traction

Snake moves by bunching and straightening its muscles

Rectilinear

HIGHLY STRUNG

For much of the day, this mangrove snake lies high up in a tree. In the late afternoon or early evening, it slides into action, raiding nests for birds and their young. It is a rear-fanged snake, found in mangrove swamps and near rain forests.

Life in the trees

MANY LIZARDS AND SNAKES are well adapted for life in trees and bushes. The toes of many arboreal, or tree-dwelling lizards are often equipped with well-developed claws for gripping tree trunks, or special pads for clinging to smooth leaf surfaces. These lizards and some of the tree snakes often have long tails which they twist around a branch, helping them to keep their balance. Some tree snakes have ridges on their belly scales, giving them additional anchorage. Arboreal reptiles are often found on isolated islands in the Pacific Ocean, where they almost certainly travelled on floating bits of vegetation.

FURRY FAT FLIER

Like the reptile flying aces, the flying squirrel glides rather than flies, using the folds of skin between its limbs. A very light animal, it sometimes eats so much it is unable to fly.

HOT LIPS

This tree boa from South America has heat-sensitive pits in its lips, so that it can find the roosting birds and bats on which it feeds. A stretchy body and strong tail make it particularly suited to its chosen habitat. As it climbs, it reaches up and coils itself around a branch, hauling up the rest of its body as it goes.

Coils act as anchor

FLYING ACE

This flying gecko has skin folds along its sides, legs, and tail, and it also has webbed feet. Together these act as a parachute when the lizard glides through the air. Like the flying dragons, it uses its abilities to get out of trouble or to swoop on food. The skin colour and texture make the gecko difficult to detect when it sits on tree bark.

HANGING ON
An emerald green tree boa catches a bird. The snake uses a branch to support itself as it makes the kill.

COOLING DOWN
The trinket snake from India is a part-time tree-dweller. In hot weather it stays on the ground, sheltering in termite mounds or under rocks. However, in cooler weather it prefers to move up into trees and bushes. Although harmless to humans, it can look quite frightening if threatened, swelling its neck, and vibrating its tail as it strikes.

Garden lizard

BLOODSUCKER
The garden lizard's body is rather like a chameleon's, and its tail is very long and slender. It can change colour rapidly, especially its head, which may turn red. In fact, the lips of some species become so red that they have been nicknamed "bloodsuckers".

DAREDEVIL DRAGONS
Flying dragons have the same gifts in the air as the flying geckos, only their "wings" are flaps of skin stretched over elongated ribs. The wings fold back along the sides of the animal when not in use.

DAY DUTY
Geckos are all good climbers, as the friction pads on the toes allow them to tackle almost any surface. This gecko is fairly unusual in that it is active by day, while most geckos are active at night. Although day geckos eat a variety of insects and soft fruit, some seem to like the nectar that they find in palm flowers.

Waterproofed

ALTHOUGH REPTILES ARE MAINLY land animals, several groups live successfully in the water. Crocodilians, a few lizards (such as the marine iguanas of the Galapagos Islands), some snakes (like the giant anaconda of South America), and terrapins and turtles all spend much of their lives submerged. Most reptiles have to return to dry land to lay their eggs, or the eggs would drown, but some sea snakes, mainly found in the oceans around Asia, northern Australia, and the Pacific Islands, get around the problem by giving birth to live young that are immediately ready to swim and able to come up for air. Different reptiles make different uses of their watery home. The crocodilians swim, hunt, and cool off in it. The marine iguanas dive in to feed on algae growing on the submerged rocks.

TAIL WALKING
If a crocodile is being chased, or if it is giving chase, it can move very fast, even leaping out of the water. This "tail walk", rather like that of the dolphins, demonstrates how graceful and at ease the animal is in water.

SNORKEL SNOUT
When an alligator dives, special muscles and flaps close over the nostrils and ears, and in calm waters it needs to keep only its nose disc above the surface. Another extra flap at the back of the throat stops the lungs from being flooded when the alligator opens its mouth under water. Its eyes are also waterproofed because they are protected by well-developed upper and lower lids, as well as by a transparent third shield which covers the eye.

Eyes placed high on the head

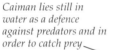

Caiman lies still in water as a defence against predators and in order to catch prey

Caiman

JESU CRISTO LIZARD

When frightened, this little basilisk lizard drops onto the water from riverside trees and bushes. It then swiftly scuttles across the surface on its back legs. Its feet have a very broad sole, and the fringe of scales on its toes gives extra support. As the lizard loses speed, it falls through the surface of the water and either swims or dives, coming up for air further on.

Basilisk lizard

MONSTERS OF THE DEEP

Humans have always believed that deep waters house strange creatures. Even today, many people believe in the existence of a monster in Scotland's Loch Ness. The extraordinary appearance of some water reptiles probably accounts for the myths that have grown up about them over the centuries.

THE WET LOOK

People are less well adapted than many reptiles to survival in the water. Unlike reptiles, our skin needs protection if we are not going to suffer from the effects of cold temperatures.

SOFT BACKS

Water turtles generally have lower, more streamlined shells than land turtles, and are therefore better suited to swimming. These soft-shelled turtles are the flattest of them all, and so are the perfect shape for hiding beneath the sand and mud on the bottom of their watery home (pp. 30–31). Unlike their land relatives, their feet have long toes that are joined by a fleshy web. This gives them extra thrust as they move through the water.

The speed of the basilisk allows it to run on the surface of the water

Nostrils lie just above water level

WATER BABY

This young caiman is very well adapted for life in the water. Its eyes, nostrils and ears are placed high on its head, so that it can still breathe and see as it lies unseen in the water. This is an advantage when hunting prey, or coming to the water's edge to drink. Not surprisingly, the caiman, like all the other crocodilians, is a good swimmer. At high speed, it can tuck its legs and webbed feet against its sides, and propel itself forward using its powerfully muscled tail. The caiman depends on water to such an extent, that if exposed to the hot sun without water nearby for a regular dip, it will die.

UNDERWATER BREATHING

All turtles have lungs, but aquatic types can also breathe through their skin, and the lining of the throat. Some can tolerate very low oxygen levels and can survive for weeks under water, but this little red-eared terrapin can last for no more than two or three hours without surfacing.

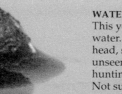

Red-eared terrapin

Best of enemies

REPTILES HAVE A NUMBER OF NATURAL ENEMIES. Large birds, such as owls and eagles, and some mammals, such as hedgehogs, pigs, and cats, all prey on snakes and lizards. Some reptiles eat their own kind; the Asian king cobra and king snakes from the USA are specialists in eating other snakes. Monitor lizards also frequently eat smaller reptiles. But the greatest enemies of reptiles are humans. Crocodiles, snakes, and lizards are still killed for their skins. Snakes are also captured so their venom can be used for medical research (pp. 42–43), and killed because they are so feared.

RIKKI-TIKKI-TAVI
In 1894, the British author Rudyard Kipling wrote *The Jungle Book* and created a hero in a little mongoose, Rikki-Tikki-Tavi. This little mammal lived with a British family in India, and became their protector, killing first Karait, a lethal krait snake, and then Nag, a cobra. The strength of the cobra is of little use to it, once the mongoose has managed to grasp the back of the snake's head.

When the hood is extended, the "eye" is meant to terrify aggressors

The snake's body is bunched ready for attack

Hood spread in attack

ENEMY NUMBER ONE
One of the most famous enemies of many snakes, but in particular the cobra, is the mongoose. In any fight, the mongoose is likely to be the victor, relying on its speed and agility to avoid the lunges of the snake. The mongoose will dart in, and bite the back of the snake's neck, or it may grab the back of the snake's head until the snake gives up the struggle. Mongooses were introduced into the West Indies in an attempt to reduce snake numbers. However, they themselves have become worse pests, attacking small animals and poultry.

THE KING
Lions are known to prey on crocodiles, even adult ones. On land, the speed and power of the mammal are enough to overcome the more sluggish reptile, although the outcome might be very different in or near water.

Stiff hairs on the back of the mongoose are raised as added protection

Razor-sharp teeth attack the cobra behind the head

Body lightly poised on back paws for quick movement

FEET FIRST

The secretary bird disturbs possible prey by stamping its feet and flapping its wings. When a snake shows itself, the bird quickly kicks at it or stamps on it, at the same time covering the snake with its wings to stop it manoeuvring into a position where it can defend itself. In this way, it can even deal with dangerous snakes such as adders and cobras. If stamping does not work, then the bird will carry the snake high into the air and drop it onto hard ground.

WAR DANCE

In Indian mythology, the demon Kaliya changed himself into a cobra and killed many herdsmen in his search for the god Krishna. Finally, Krishna killed Kaliya, then danced on his head.

TARZAN TRIUMPHS!

Tarzan the jungle hero, has no difficulty overpowering his reptilian enemy. In real life, a struggle between a crocodile and a human could have a very different ending. Although crocodiles are not usually man-eaters, they will certainly attack anyone foolish enough to stray near crocodile- infested rivers or breeding grounds.

Just good friends

Cleaner fish

Because the majority of reptiles are meat-eaters (pp. 38–39), the relationship between them and most other animals, even other reptiles, is usually that of predator and prey. However, a number of reptiles live side by side in a way that harms neither partner. Lizards and snakes, for example, together use termite mounds as incubators for their eggs. The gopher tortoise of the USA makes a burrow that is sometimes as much as 12 m (40 ft) long. This deep, cool burrow provides a permanent home for many other animals, as well as a temporary hiding place for still more. Other tortoise burrows have been recorded, where opossums, racoons, rabbits, lizards, and rats live together happily. Even rattlesnakes are said to live peacefully with the other inhabitants in such a home.

A HELPING HAND

The tuatara's existence on the remote islands off New Zealand is largely made possible by sea birds such as petrels and shearwaters (pp. 36–37). In fact, the tuatara sometimes shares its burrow with these birds. They cover the rocks and ground with their droppings, creating a perfect environment for large numbers of insects, including beetles and crickets, the tuatara's favourite food. However, it is rather an uneasy relationship, as tuataras eat nestling birds rather than insects if they get the chance.

Tuatara

Shearwater

A FRIEND INDEED

The African helmeted turtles clean tiny parasites from hippopotamuses and rhinoceroses that enter their watering holes. This cleaning behaviour is not uncommon. Some turtles are known to use their jaws to pull algae from other turtles' shells – and then they change places.

Hippopotamus

African helmeted turtle

THREE'S NOT A CROWD

All sorts of reptiles occasionally find themselves living side by side, often for different reasons. The hinge-back tortoise dislikes the dry weather of the African grasslands and hides in its burrow from the hot sun until the rainy season begins. The house snake may be investigating the same burrow for its favourite food, rats and mice, while the skink may have scuttled in to hide from an enemy. But it had better watch out. House snakes eat skinks if there is a shortage of rodents!

SLEEPING PARTNERS

Birds are sometimes said to pluck scraps of food and parasites from the gaping mouths of crocodiles. There is some doubt whether birds such as plovers would risk this, but it is true that some wander, apparently quite safely, among sleeping crocodiles. Some birds, such as the water dikkop, nest near crocodiles, and are indirectly protected by, and protect, their fearsome neighbours. Few animals will attack the birds while the crocodiles are nearby, and the birds' alarmed reaction at the approach of an enemy, in turn acts as an early warning device to the reptiles.

CLEANING UP

Many animals, outside the reptile world, live in such a way that in helping others, they also help themselves. An amazing example is the cleaner fish. It picks parasites and fragments of food off bigger fish. Here a tiny cleaner is grooming a huge fish in Australia's Barrier Reef.

An eye to the future

Snake skin wallets

UNLESS WE CHANGE THE WORLD we live in, many reptiles may face extinction. Although it has taken over 150 million years for the once immensely varied reptiles to be reduced to just four groups, these now face a greater threat than ever before. The main cause for concern lies in the terrible destruction of their natural habitats. Many reptiles have specially adapted to life in some of the areas that are being lost at a frightening rate – for example the rain forests in the tropics and much of the heathland of Europe. Although governments are now more aware of the situation and have agreed to help some severely threatened species, too little may have been done too late.

SOUP, SOUP, BEAUTIFUL SOUP
In some areas, reptiles are still very popular as a food for humans. Just a few years ago in the Caribbean, 5,000 marine turtles were turned into 682,000 litres (150,000 gallons) of soup by just one food firm.

SAFE – FOR HOW LONG?
Although still fairly common, the giant skink of the Solomon Islands faces a problem shared by many other reptiles. Its habitat is being rapidly developed, and there is concern that as this happens many of these lizards will face extinction. This particular skink has further problems – it is quite commonly eaten in some areas. A very large animal, it spends nearly all its life harmlessly enough in trees, as its monkey-like tail suggests. Mainly active at night, its diet is chiefly leaves.

TOURIST TRAP
This beautiful beach is one of the last nesting sites in Turkey of loggerhead turtles. Threatened by building programmes as a result of the tourist trade, these marine turtles face a very uncertain future, despite their long and varied history.

Baby big-headed turtle

BIG HEAD
The head of this turtle (well-named the big-headed turtle) is so large that it cannot be withdrawn into its shell. It is not yet acknowledged as being especially endangered, but because it looks so strange, it is often captured for the pet trade or used to make souvenirs. It lives in Southeast Asia, where during the day it spends its time buried in the gravel or under rocks in cool mountain streams.

An old engraving shows the head size in proportion to the body

Dirty dealing

In some parts of the world conservationists are trying to save reptiles, but many are still slaughtered to provide skins for the leather trade and souvenirs for tourists. It is a sickening market that uses the head of a hatchling as a keyring. Thousands of other reptiles have been collected by the pet trade, although in a few instances, successful captive-breeding programmes have helped to maintain the existence of rare species (pp. 36–37).

Siamese crocodile head keyring

Rattlesnake boot

UNHAPPY PET

The Pacific Island boa is found in a variety of habitats on the Solomon Islands, such as forests, farms, and near human dwellings. Like the giant skink, the main danger to its existence is the threat to its habitat. Although chiefly a ground snake, it can climb well and is sometimes found in tree hollows, living on young lizards, rodents, and birds. However, this snake is sometimes kept as a pet, which is unfortunate, because in captivity it often "sulks" and refuses to eat.

DOWN THE LADDER

Snakes are probably disappearing faster then any other group of vertebrates. They are at greater risk than ever in the 20th century, constantly in danger of being run over by cars. If something is not done to help them soon, we may be left with only board games and decorative models to remind us of these amazing animals.

Bead snake made by prisoners of war in 1916

Index

Acknowledgements

Dorling Kindersley would like to thank:
Trevor Smith and all the staff at Trevor Smith's Animal World for their help and enthusiasm.
Cyril Walker at the Natural History Museum for pages 8 and 9.
Keith Brown, Isolde McGeorge and Chester Zoo for their kind permission to photograph tuataras.

Picture credits
t=top b=bottom l=left r=right c=centre

A.N.T./P & M Walton/N.H.P.A.: 10br; 56tl
Ancient Art & Architecture Collection: 34b
Aquila Photographics: 60ml
Ardea: /J.A. Bailey 22tr; /Jean-Paul Ferrero 48br
E.N. Arnold: 14bl
Biofotos/S.Summerhays: 23tr
Bridgeman Art Library: 26b; 62ml
British Museum (Natural History): 9m
Jane Burton: 25b
© Casterman: 40tr
Bruce Coleman Ltd: 33mr; /M. Fogden 7mr; /A. Stevens 7b, 42tr, 53br; /P. Davey 14mr, 38ml; /F. Lauting 19tr; /E. Bauer 19m; /D. Hughes 21b; /J. & D. Bartlett 28l; /C. Ott 33br; /J. Burton 38tl; /G. Zeisler 41ml; /B. Wood 42m; /J. Foote 42bc, 62tl; /R. Williams 46bm; /L. Lee Rue III 56tr; /M. Brulton 62-3; /C. Frith 62t
Dorling Kindersley: 24m
Mary Evans Picture Library: 7tr; 8tl; 17tl; 18tl; 27tr; 38mr; 40mr; 43tl; 50-1;

57tm; 58tl
Sally & Richard Greenhill: 24mr
Robert Harding Picture Library: 14br; 16t; 47tl; 57mr
Michael Holford: 30tl; 34tr
Kobal Collection: 43tm
Frank Lane Picture Agency: 60m
Musee National d'Histoire Naturelle, Paris: 30ml
National Museum of Wales: 30mr
N.H.P.A.: 57ml; 61tm
Natural Science Photos: /P.H. & S.L. Ward 32
Oxford Scientific Films: 52tl; 61tl; /S. Osolinski 18m; /K. Atkinson 37br; /Z. Leszczynski 41mr, 46bl; /J. Gerlach 42bl; /Stouffer Productions 54m; /S. Mills 62br
Planet Earth Pictures: 60tl; 61br; /K. Lucas 20m; /P. Scoones 37tr
Ann Ronan Picture Library: 22bm
South Kensington Antiques: 62bc
Frank Spooner Pictures: 28br
Syndication International: 6ml
By Courtesy of the Board of Trustees of the Victoria & Albert Museum: 34m
Wildlight Photo Agency/Oliver Strewe: 21tr
Jerry Young: 42c, 43c

Illustrations by Andrew Macdonald:
13; 17; 21; 38; 41; 42; 47; 51; 53